SCOTLAND'S PAST IN ACTION

D0767123

Going to
School

Donald J Withrington

N·M·S

NATIONAL MUSEUMS OF SCOTLAND

Published by NMS Publishing
National Museums of Scotland
Chambers Street, Edinburgh EHI IJF

ISBN 0 948636 89 0

A catalogue record for this book is available from the
British Library

Series editor Iseabail Macleod
Series design by NMS Publishing
Designed by Janet Watson

Printed on Fineblade 115 gsm. Pulp from managed sustainable forests,
bleaching process elemental chlorine free

Printed in Great Britain by BPC Wheatons Ltd, Exeter

Acknowledgements

Many are influential, some unknowingly, in making even a wee book: special
thanks are due in this case to Iseabail Macleod and Colin Maclean, for good
advice and patient support readily given.

Illustrations: Front cover, ii bottom, iii top: National Gallery of Scotland. Back
cover, ii top: Trustees of the National Library of Scotland. 4, 74: Biggar
Museum Trust. 8, 10, 15, 17, 22, 24, 29, 32, 38, 42, 43, i bottom, iii bottom,
49, 51, 53, 58, 59, 60, 62, 65, 68, 80: NMS. 12: Porteous Wood. 36: University
of Glasgow Library. 41: Ayr Academy. i top: Edinburgh City Libraries. iv top:
Dundee City Council Arts and Heritage Department. iv bottom: The Board of
Trustees of the National Museums & Galleries on Merseyside. 56, 63, 65, 67,
77: Museum of Education Scotland Street School. 69, 72, 75: By kind permission of the City of Edinburgh Council Education Department. 71: MacGrory
Collection, Argyll and Bute District Libraries.

Front cover: *Detail from* A Schule Skailin *by Sir George
Harvey, 1806-76.*

Back cover: *The only known copy of a Gaelic grammar for
schools, printed in the 1870s.*

CONTENTS

INTRODUCTION

Why does 'society' want to see its youth schooled? Do the reasons offered change over time? Who, in any case, is 'society'? – the state? the churches? the parents? the local community? Who was to provide and maintain the schools? Above all, perhaps, who should pay? Whose interests were to be served by what was taught, and to whom it was taught? Who appointed teachers, provided salaries, erected school buildings, set the fees to be demanded, supervised the day-to-day working of the schools? How many and what kinds of schools were needed – for different age-ranges of pupils, for girls or for boys, for remote country areas or for thriving and populous towns? These are only some of the issues which reverberated throughout the history of education in Scotland, and found their own Scottish answers.

An early twentieth-century science class, possibly at Biggar High School. SLA

1 Early days

It is tempting to begin the story of Scottish education with the Reformation in the mid-sixteenth century, for that was a time of intended new beginnings, with many declarations of policy and of new, preferred practice. And we shall shortly come to them. But there were of course schools in Scotland before then: certainly some thriving burgh grammar schools, some monastic schools, and song schools which were attached to cathedrals and collegiate churches. A town of importance, such as Stirling in 1557, not only had its grammar school (then rivalling, in the classical languages, standards that its former pupils would find when they went to Glasgow University) but also schools for 'bairns', of both sexes, six years old and less, who were taught to 'reid and write and lay compt'. The Stirling grammar school, meanwhile, intended for the older boys in the burgh and its hinterland, taught not only Latin and Greek but also offered instruction in Hebrew, mathematics, and logic with rhetoric –here overlapping with the earlier years of the university arts curriculum. Nor was Stirling unique in this among the leading burgh schools of the time: the masters in Aberdeen and Dunbar, for instance, were also offering similarly extensive curricula. The song schools, mainly erected to train choristers for the major churches, taught reading and writing in addition to musical skills, but to very limited numbers of boys.

What is not so easy to determine is either the spread or quality of the schooling which was available in the rural parishes of Scotland in pre-Reformation days: the records are often too sparse and uninformative. But there could be much truth in the widespread complaints, by the religious reformers, that in general the rural areas were poorly served in schooling. Certainly, pre-Reformation reports from Catholic sources indicated that there had been a notable decline in school instruction outside the major Scottish towns.

In 1560 the Protestant reformers in Scotland, still very weak in the numbers and in the social standing of their declared supporters, felt obliged to produce a manifesto of their aims and policies: in a remarkable document called the *Book of Discipline,* as well as outlining vital areas of theology and religious practice in which they wanted to see changes introduced, they spelled out the duties and responsibilities which, as a citizen, the individual owed to the state – or, more correctly, to that alliance of church and state which they called the 'godly commonwealth' – and also the responsibilities which the community, local and national, should bear towards individual citizens. In what was intended to be seen as the reformers' new contract with the nation, much attention was given to impressing on each locality in the land (through the new parish minister it was to have, through the new kirk session it was to form, and through the local gentry acting as 'godly magistrates') the need to provide for the moral and social improvement of the people. For three centuries the *Book of Discipline* was to remain a constant reference point in Scotland in all matters of social policy, particularly in the provision of poor relief and schooling.

The reformers' plan of education is very revealing. Each parish was to be assured of a local school to teach all the children who were of school age (varyingly interpreted as five or six or seven to ten or eleven) reading, writing and arithmetic, and where possible Latin too. Children from distant country areas where the local community found they could not attract or support a Latin teacher were, 'if apt to learning', to be sent to a nearby grammar school (which implies that boys alone were here being considered): from there, with others of ability whose parents wished them to continue their education, they would move to the nearest large town, to a regional centre which was to have a college of liberal arts. These colleges, at which the sons of poorer families would be supported by bursaries, were intended to provide more advanced instruction in Latin and Greek, perhaps also teaching of Hebrew, logic and rhetoric. The educational structure was to be completed with the three universities of St Andrews, Glasgow and Old Aberdeen (King's College) which would teach dialectics, mathematics, physics, moral philosophy, ethics and politics, leading to 'postgraduate' degrees in divinity, law and medicine. The reformers expected the whole structure to be very substantially paid for out of the inherited wealth of the old church.

Elementary schooling for all, girls and boys alike, was the means to salvation: no longer to be gained through the intercession of priests or saints, but by a justification of faith achieved by an individual and personal reading of the Scriptures (to be widely available in Scots for this purpose). A crucial aid in these personal studies was to be found in the hearing of, and close attention to, the interpretative sermons of the new, reformed ministry; hence

The University of Glasgow in the late seventeenth century.
From John Slezer's Theatrum Scotiae, *1690.*

the insistence that all parishioners, including school pupils, should attend church services.

For the talented male scholars in the local communities, poorer and richer, there was to be the opportunity to progress to the limits of their abilities in what was to be a coherent, 'end-on' system of elementary, advanced and higher education. At all stages two interests were to be served: those of each individual, striving to assure his or her salvation; and the interests of the 'common good' or the 'common weal', local and national. Community interests, the benefit of the nation in church and state, were to have at all times greater weight than personal desires. Thus, as is made plain in the *Book of Discipline:* ' this must be carefully provided, that no father, of what estate or condition that ever he be, use his children at his own fantasy, especially in their youth-head; but all must be compelled to bring up their children in learning and virtue. . . If they be found apt to letters and learning, then they may not (we mean neither the sons of the rich nor yet the sons of the poor) be permitted to reject learning, but must be charged to continue their study, so that the Commonwealth may have some comfort by them'.

The wealth of the old church did not fall into the hands of the Protestant reformers, and so the parishes, in the first instance, were left to fend for themselves as best they could. What is remarkable is that they did this, generally, to great effect. Quite extraordinarily, at least in Lowland Scotland, parish after parish seems to have been able to engage and maintain public school-masters (and frequently, where needed, additional teachers, male and female, to teach the rudiments to those living at too great a distance to attend the funded parochial school).

The 1560 plan had to be amended elsewhere too, in order to suit the new conditions. In the burghs, lacking the hoped-for endowment which would have converted their main schools into liberal arts colleges, the town councils put much effort into providing their citizens with classical grammar schools of quality, and in addition ABC schools (as they were often called) teaching

Edinburgh's original High School, built in 1578.

reading and writing and perhaps some arithmetic. And the educational structure was then completed by not three, but five, universities – the two additions, the 'town's college' of Edinburgh given degree-granting rights in 1582, and Marischal College and University founded in 1592 in New Aberdeen. These five universities in their turn would retain the teaching of the whole of the old arts curriculum, as well as providing postgraduate teaching for the main professions. Hence, by the beginning of the seventeenth century, one of the lasting and most distinctive features of the Scottish educational system had been brought into place: namely, the direct linkage of local schools (in country or in town) with the nation's universities, as a way of ensuring access to higher education. That this university instruction was generally cheaper at the local university – with the students close to home – would ensure another distinctively Scottish characteristic: the strongly regional catchments from which Scottish universities drew their students.

2 Consolidation

The early decades of Reformed Scotland were difficult and insecure. Local congregations alone provided its educational and other resources, and there were many calls on them. As early as 1562 the general assembly petitioned the Scottish parliament for aid in supporting schoolmasters at the parish churches; for not only were the schools 'requisite for erecting of a perfect reformed kirk' but, as was noted in 1587, were 'necessary instruments to come to the true meaning and sense of the will of God revealed in his word', thus forming good citizens for the state. But, apart from some grants from chantry funds (often in the form of bursaries to named recipients to attend burgh schools or universities), very little was done. Parishes and burghs were thrown back on to their own intiatives. Their commitment to the new ideals was soon very evident. Even by the end of the sixteenth century, at least for those areas of the Lowlands for which we have records, fair progress had been made. Parliament found it had to act to ensure provision for the parochial poor, instituting a local taxation assessed on 'means and substance' instead of having to rely on charitable givings alone, and transferring the administration of poor relief into the hands of the minister and kirk session of each locality, but no similar move was made for education. And that implies that additional support of this kind, from the centre, was seen to be unnecessary.

Indeed, by the early years of the seventeenth century when church records, including those of the recently formed presbyteries, become rather more numerous, there is good evidence that in the majority of Lowland parishes there was schooling of some kind. In many parishes of such counties as East Lothian and Fife, we know that schools had probably been in operation for some time. And not any schooling would do: parish after parish, even in remote parts of the country, strained to have Latin grammar taught in its school, as a matter of status and self-respect; this also always had the advantage of relieving parents of the expense of boarding out their boys elsewhere. Thus, when a vacancy occurred in 1615 in a small and sparsely populated parish such as Tyninghame in East Lothian, the minister and session can be found rejecting candidates because, after due examination, they were thought incapable of teaching Latin or teaching it to the standard required. The parishioners of Tyninghame were by no means alone in their quest.

That being the case, we have to account for the fact that in the early decades of the seventeenth century the state (monarchy and parliament alike) became remarkably active in the cause of school provision in Scotland. In 1616 the privy council passed an act, intended to press localities without schools to provide at once for them, and this act was renewed and added to by parliament in 1633. If local agencies were, so generally as we have surmised, already and effectively at work, then why these bursts of activity? The answer lies in both instances in crises in the political situation. There was rebellion in the western Highlands and in the

George Heriot's School, Edinburgh, showing the handsome frontage of the original seventeenth-century school. Porteous Wood

Hebrides, and government saw in schooling (which in the right hands would be able to inculcate there more acceptable Lowland ways) a long-term solution to its problems. The terminology of the 1616 intervention by the privy council reveals all:

> Forsamekle as the kingis Majestie haveing a speciall care and regaird that the trew religion be advanceit and establisheit in all pairts of the kingdome, and that all his Majesties subjects, especially the youthe, be exercised and trayned up in civilitie, godlines, knawledge and learning, that the vulgar Inglische tongue be universallie plantit and the Irishe language, whilk is one of the cheif and principall caussis of the continewance of barbaritie and incivilitie amongis the inhabitants of the Isles and Heylandis, may be abolisheit and removit; and quhairas thair is no meane more powerful to further this his Majesties princelie regaird and purpois than the establisheing of scooles in the particular parrocheis of this kingdome whair the youthe may be taught at the leist to write and reid and be catechised and instructed in the groundis of religioun; thairfore the kingis Majestie, with the advise of the Lords of his Secreit Counsall, hes thocht it necessar and expedient that in everie parroch of this kingdome whair convenient meanes may be had for interteyning a scoole, that a scoole salbe establisheit, and a fit person appointit to teach the same, upoun the expensis of the parrochinnaris according to the quantitie and qualitie of the parroche, at the sight and be the advise of the bischop of the diocie in his visitatioun. . .

There was nothing new in this attempt to break the hold of the Gaelic language and of the law and culture of Gaeldom. In 1598 James VI had written of the need to 'plant' Lowlanders or the more amenable of the mainland Highlanders among the rebellious Islesmen (much as he was to do later in Ulster to quell rebellion and supplant the old leadership there). And in 1609 he demanded that all the sons of the chieftains of clans in the Highlands and Western Isles should be brought south to be educated in the Lowlands so that they might return, break with old and barbarous ways, and introduce the king's law and 'civilised' living into their lands. In fact, the privy council act of 1616 was only another, if longer-term move, extended this time to include all the inhabitants in his proposed changes, to incorporate these awkward areas into the Scottish (indeed, into the British) state. Educational policy ran in parallel with other government moves, to plant and settle Protestant ministers in the furthest-flung parishes of 'barbarous' Gaeldom. Especially worrying crises on the western seaboard, in 1613-16 and again in 1630-33, were the real stimulus to the 1616 act and then to its repetition and renewal by parliament in 1633.

However, one part of the text in 1616 was to be of very general importance, in the Lowlands and elsewhere, in attempts to improve the provision of schooling; it introduced, formally, a principle which was to be another distinctive mark of the Scottish parochial school system for centuries afterwards. The responsibility for 'entertaining' a school and for providing a basic stipend to the schoolmaster was not to be that of the parents alone, but was to be laid directly on all the parishioners. Thus, in other words, the provision of schooling was quite specifically to be made a community function, something to be supported by all, whether or not they had children, whether or not they were likely to receive some personal or family benefit from the service. And in 1633 parliament made only one substantive addition to this privy council act: a 'stent', that is a local tax, levied on all land according to its worth, was to be paid by the heritors (landowners) and the tenants who owned or rented that land, 'for the maintenance and establishing of the saidis schools'. If the heritors failed to agree, then ' the consent of the most pairt of the parischioners' alone would put it into legal operation.

The 1620s, 1630s and 1640s were intermittently, but frequently, times of dearth and destitution in Scotland. Complaints were to be heard, not least from schoolteachers, that in harsh years many parishes found much difficulty in fulfilling their public duties in social welfare, in poor relief and in supporting education. In 1638-39, the national church (at the beginning of a period of presbyterian ascendancy) can be found pleading with government to act to secure continuity of schooling and its better maintenance throughout the land – no doubt also having in mind the added value of these schools as a means of 'breeding' the next generation in the 'true' covenanted religion. Stipends, it was claimed, were too often both 'litle and ill payed', as a result forcing masters to leave their posts in order to find a living elsewhere if they could. By 1646, in the aftermath of a time of particular distress, we hear of a 'prejudicial want of schools in manie congregations'. In that year parliament came again to the rescue.

The 1646 act required the founding of a school and the appointment of a schoolmaster 'in everie paroche (not alreadie provyded)' – a parenthesis which shows that there was certainly no universal lack of schooling. In many respects, indeed, the act intentionally built on what had already been put in place. While reminding parishioners of their obligations, it also tightened up the duties which had been laid on them. They were, thenceforth, to build 'a commodious house' for a school; they were to pay an assured and stated stipend to the master (his basic salary, to which he would add the payments for fees) of not less than 100 merks – 100 x 13s 4d (66.7p) – and not more than 200 merks;

A seventeenth-century schoolhouse (now a Masonic Lodge) in South Queensferry, West Lothian. SLA

and they were to raise this money by an agreed stent on 'stock and teind, proportionallie to worth'. The vaguenesses of earlier acts had gone: the erection and maintenance of a school were no longer dependent on 'convenient meanes' being available; and not only was a minimum stipend instituted, a maximum was introduced in order to stop larger and richer parishes tempting teachers away from smaller and poorer regions.

But this act was to have a relatively short life. In 1661, along with other legislation passed in the period of interregnum before the restoration of the monarchy under Charles II, it was deleted from the statute book – leaving the less specific 1633 act as the legal standard for school provision. Nonetheless, local church records for the next thirty years show that in many districts stipends of at least 100 merks were raised from the stenting of parish lands, and often schoolhouses were built: bishops, indeed, were remarkably active in Lowland areas in the 1660s and 1670s (and, for instance, in Argyll too) in visiting their dioceses, and enquiring directly into the state of the parish schools. In 1696, after the Revolution and the final establishment of presbyterianism in church government, and in yet another time of famine and crisis, parliament revived the more exacting provisions of the 1646 legislation, and these became the legal basis for the Scottish parochial school system until the nineteenth century. The 1696 act, indeed, was for long regarded as the 'magna carta' of Scottish education, on the false presumption that it would have been passed only if the previous legislation had been ineffective. But the educational heritage of the *Book of Discipline* to the seventeenth century, for all the political and religious upsets of that era, was both more substantial and more continuous than has often been imagined.

There is now sufficient evidence for the amount of schooling available in Scotland, in the course of the seventeenth century, for some general estimates to be made. In the central Lowlands, at least half of the parishes had schoolteachers by the 1640s; by the 1670s, that proportion rises to some 70 per cent or more; and by the early 1690s it is close to 90 per cent, a figure which may still prove to be overcautious. The sheer spread of this schooling, with larger and more populous parishes sometimes supporting more than one school, is very remarkable. Moreover, in the counties of the Lothians and Fife at least, nine-tenths of those parish schools we know were in existence in the early 1690s were grammar schools; they had teachers in post who could instruct their pupils in Latin, so keeping open the possibility of their going on to university.

Nor does the picture in some Highland areas seem to be so different. If we consider only the Gaelic-speaking parishes of Perthshire and of Highland Banffshire, then once again by the 1670s we find some 70 per cent had schools, and by the 1690s they matched the 90 per cent we found in south-eastern Scotland. Certainly, north of the Great Glen the evidence is much thinner and that itself may reflect a rather different situation. And yet

Mingulay schoolhouse, Barra, photographed by Alasdair Alpin Macgregor, probably in the 1920s. SLA

there is still plenty of information for individual parishes there, as also in the Inner and Outer Hebrides. Island communities such as those in Bute or Mull or Skye were well served; and we know of schools of some quality in Stornoway in Lewis and in Rodel in Harris in the later seventeenth century. Mainland districts, such as Badenoch and Lochaber, had a good spread of schooling; but there are many fewer parishes with known schools in Wester Ross or Sutherland. Whether or not districts were predominantly Gaelic-speaking seems not to have been a major, or a defining, factor. However, those parts of the Highlands and Islands in which the post-Reformation church (presbyterian or episcopal) had been well and strongly established are generally those for which the evidence for school provision is also strong. Thus, their ecclesiastical condition might well be the most crucial influence in whether or not Highland parishes had schools. It is not until presbyterian ministers were permanently settled in those regions of the Highlands and Islands for which the seventeenth-century evidence is most thin, in the aftermath of both the Revolution and the parliamentary Union of 1707, that we find surer indications of the presence of public schoolmasters there.

3 Quality and style in early schooling

Merely providing a salary for a schoolteacher, and perhaps a schoolhouse in which to teach (though for many parishes the church itself was used), were not the limits of the responsibility of the heritors, minister and kirk session; the schoolteacher had to be supervised and the type, content and character of the schooling had to be managed. At their appointment schoolteachers were often asked to agree to the particular conditions of service then offered. These might allow or forbid the teacher to act also as clerk to the kirk session and/or precentor (that is, the person leading the singing in the church); they would often specify the subjects to be taught and the fees to be exacted; they might set down the holidays to be observed; and so on. Now and again, a new appointment was the occasion for parishes to adopt (sometimes quite elaborate) sets of school rules. A set of rules might be recommended to all its parishes by a presbytery, as known guidelines to schoolmaster and parish alike of what would be specifically scrutinized at a forthcoming parochial visitation. For the historian, these rules can provide an interesting glimpse of the day-to-day working of seventeenth-century parochial schools.

The parish of Dundonald in Ayrshire provides us with an extraordinarily full account, as early as 1640, of the 'orders to be subscribed be him who shall have charge of instructing the youth heirefter'. Other sets of rules which have survived include those for groupings of parishes in East Lothian in 1673, for Aberdeenshire in 1675, and for Highland presbyteries in Perthshire and Stirlingshire in 1698; they indicate clearly that something very like a standardized contract emerged during the century but one which, interestingly, might sometimes include clauses that reflected particular difficulties with existing or recently removed local schoolmasters. The general oversight of the parochial schools was certainly left in Church hands, but other agencies could be called in for support, perhaps to secure the regular attendance of children 'come to age' as was done in East Lothian: 'if anie cannot be moved by the intreatie of the min[iste]r to put ther children to school, ther superiors, heritors or magistrates of the place, is desired to interpose ther authoritie for that effect'.

Frequently we can find much about the internal organization of the local schools from such rules, including curriculum and timetabling, the recommended styles of teaching, as well as other duties specified to the master. We find, for example, that the school day was expected to be a long one (but with some allowance made in winter for the very young and those living at a distance). The Dundonald regulations of 1640 spell it all out for an incoming master:

4. Let the childrein in the moneths of October, November, December, Januar, Februar, meit in the morning at the sunne

ryssing and be dismissed at the sunne setting at nicht, except some younger ones or those quho ar farder distant from the shoole, of quhom some consideratioun must be had. All the rest of the yeir let the hour of gathering in the morning be seaven of clock and the hour of skailing six, and such as leirns Latein wold always prevent the rest a prettie space.

5. Let the shollers goe to breckfast at 9 hours and convein againe at 10; to dinner lykewayes at 12 hours and returne at one afternoone, so neir as may be; for quilk purpose thair must be a sand glasse to measour the hours. . .

15. And because mony, far lesse the tender youth, ar unable to abyde continuall bensill [pressure] of learning let them have for preserving and sharpning thair engynes [ingenuity, minds] some recreatioun on the ordinar days, Tuysday, Thursday and Saturday, in the efternoone for the space of one hour in the Winter, of from October to Februar, and two hours the rest of the yeir. But let the maister see that they play not at ony unlawful or obscene pastime or such other as may reddilie defyle or rent thair cloaths or hurt thair bodies; and let a convenient place be choissin neirby the shoole, but not at the churchyaird nor ony pairt of it; quhilk is dormatorium sanctum, a place for no ordinarie civill imployment, it serving for mourning rather than for playing and sporting, quhilk wold be keipit honest and separat for thair own usse.

The same timetable, more or less, was observed in the town's grammar school in Kirkcaldy in Fife according to school rules passed (more likely repeated) in 1705. Those aged seven or eight or upwards, having already learned their English reading in 'women's schools', were to attend from 7 am until 6 pm, with breaks at 9-10 and 12-2, except on Tuesdays when they were dismissed for play at 4 pm and on Saturdays at 12 noon – but were 'discharged from playing in the Town, Church Yard, in boates or shipes, or anywayes in the Sea, as also from throwing stones, or playing with the carrock on the streets [shinty], or from playing anywhere out of their houses after the 8 o'clock bell at night, either summer or winter'.

While the school day opened and closed with prayer, it was usual for the teacher to spend time on religious instruction (to 'go over the grondis of religioun') with all the pupils on Saturday forenoons, including the forms of prayer and of 'the blessings before and after meat'. In Dundonald, we find that at the close of each school day the master was to give his pupils, 'according to thair age and progresse', a nightly task: learning by heart some portion of 'the Lords Prayer, Beliefs, Commands, Graces or Catechisme', to be repeated to him before the beginning of ordinary lessons on the following day. In town and country alike, the school pupils convened again on Sundays, to go to church with their masters, sitting there together; and were to 'have in reddines quhat they have observed' on Mondays, when they would be closely examined on 'ther keiping church and attention to the sermon'.

There were attempts too to regulate the normal school day. The teaching of the whole school, in country parishes and in burghs alike, was carried on in one room – which might be 36 feet x 15 feet or as small as 20 feet x 13 feet – in which all were instructed together. In burgh schools or in the largest parish schools, which had 'doctors' or assistants to the masters, the two shared the same space. In country parish schools, the responsibility of the master to all his pupils was often underlined – to those of all ages and at all stages, whether they were learning Latin or not, whether poor or from well-heeled families. In all schools, whether held in specially-built accommodation or (quite often still) in some part of the parish church, there was usually much small-group teaching, while other scholars in the room settled to the 'tasks' which had been allotted to them earlier; at times during the day individuals would then be called forward, so that their lesson might be 'heard at the master's desk'. At least one hour per day, normally from 11 am to noon, was set aside for writing exercises, whether in Scots or in Latin.

*School at Gairney Bridge in Kincardine. Seriously dilapidated,
it still shows the schoolroom as it might have been in the
eighteenth century.* SLA

Burgh schools were usually fitted up with 'buirds' and 'formes'
for writing on and sitting on, as were the better equipped of the
larger parish schools; but country schools might have little by way
of furnishings: a master's desk and chair, some benches perhaps
(wooden, or even stone or mortar seats placed around the walls),
not always with tables or boards to lean on. Where a school had
been built as such, or another building had been well adapted for
the purpose, then it might contain two storeys, one for the schoolroom, the other as the master's dwelling. More frequently, the
master and school-doctor had 'house-mail' (or money for rental)
paid to them for whatever accommodation they could find for
themselves and their families nearby. Bespoke buildings (and
there seems to have been much school-building in the second half
of the seventeenth century) often had wooden floors and good
fireplaces; elsewhere earthen floors covered with rushes were not
uncommon. Complaints are to be found about the coldness in
winter of schools held in parish churches without any heating.

Yet few public or private schools in Fife seem to have matched the splenetic description by a prejudiced English visitor to one in Burntisland in 1677, aghast that the floor was 'strewed with grass, moss, etc., and all the boys lay there in the litter like pigs in a sty'. Even country children seem to have been able to provide themselves with stools to sit on, as well as with paper and quills and books: pleadings to heritors and kirk sessions for better buildings and equipment, understandably, often contained exaggerated descriptions of the badness of existing conditions, and we should be cautious of accepting them at face value.

Whatever might have been the physical state of the accommodation and its lack of convenience, the school rules that have survived clearly expected the parochial schoolmaster to be exacting in his attention to his primary tasks, the teaching of reading and writing. Here again are the Dundonald regulations:

12. For the childreins better profiting let those quho ar farder advanced in reiding Scottish, quither print or writ [handwriting], each of them have the charge of a yong sholler, quho shall sit besyde them, quhome they shall make perfyte of his lessoun against the tyme come he shall be called to say, on the negligent parteis, quhilk of the two soever it shall be fund to have bein; and let the elder shollers them selfs speir at [ask] the maister quhat words they ar ignorant of in thair own lessoun, it being alwayes provyded that the elder sholler his furdering of the yonger hinder not himself in his learning.

13. Let a speciall care be had of the childreins writing quho ar meit for it. Let the hour named betwixt xj and 12 be alloted to that exercise every day and forder to those whoise speciall ayme that is. Let the maister mak or mend thair pens, rule thair paper, cast thair coppes, tak inspectioun particularlie of everie ons writing, point out the faults and learn them by ocular demonstratioun in his own practeise before them how to mend. The maister must lead the hands of the yong beginners, stand over thair heid for thair directioun, and be goeing throuch all for thair furderance.

Regulations for the teaching of Latin were also quite elaborately laid down, in Dundonald and elsewhere, including the giving out of 'penses' [tasks] as homework, and instruction in prose as well as in translation. Sometimes very specific directions were laid down as to which texts and grammars were to be used. Here and there, from other evidence, it seems likely that some supplementary teaching in classics, especially for those pupils intending to go on to university, was provided by the parish minister (very often an ex-parochial master) in his manse.

But nearly all the sets of school rules make it clear that the schoolmaster's responsibilities reached well beyond the scholarly curriculum:

> 14. As the maister wold be carefull and conscientious to teach his
> shollers guid learning so wold he also learn them guid manners,
> how to carie them selfs fashionablie towards all, and for that
> purpose wold learn them gesturs of courtessie to be ussed towards
> himself in the school, thair parents at home, gentlemen, eldermen
> and others of honest fashion abroad. He wold put into thair
> mouths styls of compellatioun sutable to each ons place to quhom
> they speik, and how to compose thair countenance, eys, hands,
> feit, quhen ony speiks to them or they to them, and that they be
> taught to abandon all unciveill gesturs, as skarting [scratching] of
> the heid, armes, etc.

Hornbook, used by children learning to read and write. The name derives from the fact that the surface was protected by a thin sheet of transparent horn.

So demanded the session and minister of Dundonald. Thirty years later the presbytery of Haddington was less immediately concerned with the positive teaching of good behaviour than with the teachers' responsibility to punish bad behaviour, notably those who were 'disobedient to ther parents or irreverent in time of divine worship', while the synod of Aberdeen – also in the 1670s – required all masters to chastise their pupils 'for cursing, swearing, Lying, speakeing profanitie; for disobedience to parents and what vices appeares in them'.

Most sets of rules also have something to say about the kinds of punishment which might be meted out in school. Again, the Dundonald regulations are worth quoting:

16. And finallie as without disciplein no companie can be keipit in ordour, so leist of all unbrydled youth, therfoir it shall be necessarie that thair shall be in the shoole a common censor quho shall remark all faults and delate them to the maister, of quhom compt wold be taken once a weik; and for more perfyte understanding of the childreins behaviour thair wold be a clandestein censor of quhom none shall know bot the maister and he who is employed in that office that may secretlie acquent the maister with all things; and according to the qualitie of the faults, the maister shall inflict punishment, streking some on the leg with a birk wand, belt or pair of taws, others on the hips as thair fault deservs, bot non at ony tyme or in ony caice on the heid or cheiks. And heirin especiallie is the maister to kyth [show] his prudence in taking up the severall inclinatiouns of his shoolers and applying himself thairunto by lenitie, allurements, commendations, fair words, some littill rewards, drawing from vice and provocking to vertue such as may be won thairby, and others by moderat severitie if that be fund most convenient for thair stubbornes; and let the wyse maister rather by a grave, austere and authoritative countenance and cariage represse insolenceis and gaine everie one to thair dewtie than by stroks, yit not neglecting the rod quhair it is neidful.

The master's behaviour, as well as that of his pupils, also had a place in these wide-ranging contractual arrangements. Matters of poor time-keeping, particularly his leaving the school unattended without due notice and permission given, would prompt a minister and heritors and kirk session into action against a defaulting master. And worse faults were sometimes in mind. Spending large stretches of their teaching days in 'supplementary' careers as notaries or merchants or in running meal-mills were matters of complaint here and there, and the pursuit of such 'other avocations' was outlawed (especially if attempts were also being made by the parochial authorities to improve the masters' stipends). In the 1690s, for instance, the session and heritors of Kennoway in Fife at last addressed the years of trouble they had had with their schoolmaster, passing a set of regulations which nicely represented the core of the problem they had long had with him:

> 1st That the schoolmaster present or any who succeeds to him shall not extrude any scholar out of the school (except for two days only) untill the ground be Examined by the Session, without special advice at least of the Minister and of the Session if the difference can no otherwise be removed.

> 2nd That no Schoolmaster in office shall spend their time in hunting and gunning, that they are oblidged to attend on the School, that is, betwixt six of the cloack in the morning and six at night, except what time they are necessarily taken up in eating and drinking and other necessary affairs. . .

> 5th That no Schoolmaster in office shall spend his tyme in tavernes when he is bound to wait upon the School, and that he shall forbear to keep company with profane and vain loose livers, drunkards or swearers, or such as are vitious.

> 6th That the Schoolmaster shall not absent himself a day nor half a day from the School unless he acquaint the Minister therwith and he think his reasons are relavent and that he shall not give his Schoolers a vacancie without the special allowance of the Session.

Mr Robert Wilson, the master, confessed his faults and accepted the rebukes of session and heritors. He obviously found the rules too much for him, for a fortnight later he was reported to have 'gon away and deserted his place'.

4 A new century: reacting to customer demands

As the eighteenth century dawned, and before the coming of the parliamentary union with England in 1707, we find new and searching questions being asked about the content and styles of teaching to be found in the public schools of Scotland. In 1700 all the presbyteries within the Synod of Glasgow and Ayr were invited to give their views on how the state of education in their districts might be improved. The answers were provided by meetings of the ministers, professional men who frequently had served as schoolmasters before their ordination, and provide a revealing and sophisticated commentary on the educational situation, at least in the west of Scotland. Coming in the aftermath of a long period of disruptive famine and economic distress, which had severely reduced the security of schoolmastering as a career and had often reduced salaries, the reports noted the decline in quality of much teaching; especially the insufficiency of those who had been poorly taught the classics to teach them well, in turn, to their pupils. Better men were needed and would only be got by offering better returns for their labours. More than that, however, the question was consistently raised as to whether a curriculum restricted to reading, writing, a little arithmetic and Latin was any longer fitted to the educational needs of the country; and whether a wider choice of subjects, attracting more pupils for longer, would not engender a securer and better-rewarded living to the public schoolmasters. In its return, the presbytery of Glasgow was careful to distinguish two groups of scholars: 'those that follow their studies with a designe to gett a livelyhood in the Church or Commonwealth thereby, and those who have no such designe but have provision to maintain themselves otherwise':

that is, the able poor whose access to university study, and hence to employment at the schoolmaster's desk or in the pulpit, required the old curriculum; and those who had family backing for other careers and no need to be restricted to it. This presbytery argued that the latter group would only lose time – 'and that of their best time for learning of things that may be more usefull for them' – in the study of Latin: for them reading, writing, counting, 'some of the usefullest parts of Geometry and Geography', the psalm tunes, and 'History, especially of our own church and state' were recommended.

The presbytery of Hamilton recommended that the wider curriculum, without Latin, should be offered to everyone; and then able pupils (or those whose parents were ready to pay) should be admitted to a four- or five-year public Latin school, with Greek and Hebrew added in the fifth year. But more than the classical languages would still be taught:

> Roman and Greek Antiquities, a compend of all Trades and Sciences, Comenii Janua and Atrium, and particularly some knowledge of Geography, both by the globe and plain chart, especially the Geographia Veterum [which] were very profitable for schools and for the understanding of history and reading it with pleasure; also some elements of chronology, all which may be rendered easie and delightful by Tables, draughts and pictures.

In short, the emphasis was on two things: firstly, that what the children learned should be useful, fitting them for the particular occupations which were to be chosen for them; secondly, that that learning should be attractive and agreeable. (Note especially the recommendation to employ the 'advanced' teaching methods of Comenius, a renowned educationist in Eastern Europe.)

This rethinking of the usual curriculum may not, at least on our present evidence, have had a swift response; but the notion that education should be useful – with Latin 'useful' too for those going on, via university studies, into the professions – certainly did not disappear, nor was the suggestion that there should be options available in practical and 'modern' subjects lost to view. We know that by 1723 in Dumfries a 'writing or commercial school' was added to the grammar school there. Then in 1746 the Ayr town council split the old burgh school into three departments: of classics; of English subjects; and of science subjects (arithmetic, book-keeping, geometry, navigation, surveying, algebra and other parts of mathematical sciences, parts of natural philosophy). In Ayr it was intended that pupils would progress through the departments of study in a stated order: English; then classics; then, with:

Sampler made by Betty Pleanderleath at Mrs Seton's school in Edinburgh, 1745.

the Grammar School instructions being over, it is proposed that by employing ten months of the year in teaching, and a proper arrangement of Classes, a complete course of the other parts of Academical Education may be gone through in two years and a half, or at most in three years.

What was being implemented in Ayr was an educational structure which in its later stage offered an alternative – a modern, utilitarian alternative – to a university education. This was held to be attractive to parents for a number of reasons, including the fact of its cheapness, since their sons would not need to be sent away and boarded out, but also because it was held that a highly concentrated course of study would be preferable, morally and intellectually, to those 'speculative and indolent habits' engendered by a university course of only five or six months per year spread over four years. Many localities developed similar, but not often so elaborate, ways of widening the curriculum. In Elgin the grammar schoolmaster in 1748 advertised that, besides English, Latin and writing, 'he directs the studies of such young Lads as incline to Trades, Merchandize, etc. . . to such Branches of Education as are most adapted to the way of life they choose'. In the same year commercial and navigation schools abounded in New Aberdeen. The parochial schoolmaster at Old Deer in Aberdeenshire let it be known in 1750 that he offered 'Arithmetick, Book-Keeping after the Italian method, Geography, Geometry and Algebra, all taught at reasonable rates', in addition to Latin and English. In Kinghorn in Fife in 1763 a three-part course of navigation was taught but, as was sometimes the case elsewhere, this was held in the evenings, from 6 pm to 8 pm, and not in 'the time of the public school' (and therefore, no doubt, was open to adults also).

More and more burgh schools incorporated the new subjects into their courses, and followed the example of Perth in 1760 in adopting the title of 'academy' in order to signify to potential customers the changes which had been made. In the largest towns, however, the grammar schools remained unaltered, restricting themselves to instruction in the classics; but their timetables might allow their pupils also to attend one or more of the extraordinary spread of private establishments which sprang up locally, providing instruction at all levels in modern languages, in navigation and astronomy, in book-keeping, in music and dancing, in trigonometry and land measurement, or whatever. Customer choice tended more and more to rule the educational market. In the larger towns there were also private academies which, on the example of the earlier subscription (but still public) academy in Perth, quite clearly intended to provide a new style of university-type training, stressing the value of a structured course within one institution. Hence in Glasgow in the early 1760s:

> Attentive to the importance and utility of a judicious Plan of Education, and convinced by experience of the impropriety of many different schools for the purposes thereof, William Gordon and James Scruton have been at pains to render their Academy as complete as possible, by procuring the assistance of masters properly qualified for teaching the modern languages, which our commerce hath rendered necessary for the man of business to be acquainted with, and such of the sciences as they themselves could not (without neglecting others as essential) overtake; by which means the youth committed to their care will be instructed in every branch of literature, proper for the merchant, the mechanic, the marine and the farmer, under their own eye, the proper master being always at hand to resolve the difficulties that may occur, without the disagreeable necessity of strolling from school to school at the expiration of almost every hour.

The plan of classes in Gordon's and Scruton's Academy was very extensive. In addition to the usual and expected subjects, we find: practical geometry, plain and spherical trigonometry with their application in land surveying, longimetry, altimetry, navigation, geography, astronomy, fortification, gunnery and dialling; French; and Italian and Spanish if required. The advertisement from which this information has been gleaned also promised, if support for them was found, to employ yet more qualified masters to teach 'Rhetoric; Composition in the Latin, English, French, Spanish and Italian Language with taste and propriety'.

But the exercise of market forces, and with that some weakening of community vigilance over the local public provision of schools, could and did bring its problems – particularly in smaller parishes with less attentive or less supportive ministers and heritors. There are signs that the quality of local schooling was already under threat: in some districts the better-off were sending their children to board at attractive schools outside their parishes, while another and severe inflation in the 1780s seriously diminished the returns from teaching in poorly-attended public schools where the pupils only learned and paid for the rudiments. The problem of recruiting, and of keeping, decently qualified masters was in these instances ever present; and the probable effects were forcefully, and exaggeratedly, described in the return which the minister of St Andrew's Llanbryde in Moray (a parish

Alphabet counters made of bone.

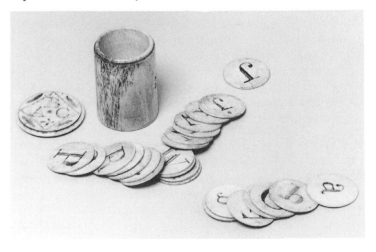

uncomfortably close to Elgin, with its readily-available spread of other schools) made to Sir John Sinclair's *Statistical Account of Scotland* in the early 1790s:

> since by the alteration of the times, the salaries of schoolmasters can in no way support a family, that, and office has fallen in to the hands of mere school-boys, which they abandon as soon as their own education is supposed to be completed, or into that of bankrupt tenants, still less qualified for the duties of it. So that a thicker cloud of ignorance must be settling over the lower ranks of the people, than that which covered their fathers. And while the reputation for learning, which Scotland has long supported among the nations, must in a short time be lost, those numbers, who, by means of that mediocrity of literature acquired in the parish schools, rose from the lowest stations of life to merit, wealth and rank, must be henceforth chained down, hopeless and inglorious, to the miserable sphere of their humble birth.

We should not, however, be misled by the Rev. William Leslie. His comments are not paralleled in the general run of ministers' replies to Sir John Sinclair. The returns to the Account, on balance, show a teaching force which, in spite of financial privations where the numbers attending were small and their scholarly requirements meagre, was intent on maintaining the old system in reasonable heart. The old parochial structure had certainly been badly weakened in the later eighteeenth century; but it was still in place, and on the whole well enough placed, once government did come to its rescue in 1803, to revive its fortunes.

Nor should it be presumed that, if bad times had struck at schooling in the Lowlands, then in the Highlands and Islands – torn apart by politics and by successive periods of famine which had prompted much emigration – the eighteenth century must have produced dire consequences for education. The assumption that the Highlands and Islands were all but bereft of schooling needs to be corrected. Reports of visitors in the mid-1750s, surveying school provision and need on behalf of the Society in Scotland for Propagating Christian Knowledge (SSPCK), allow us to survey a wide range of parishes in the Gaelic-speaking mainland and the Western and Northern Isles: out of a total of 105 parishes, at least 88 (or 84 per cent) certainly had public schools supported by heritors and tenants. Such parochial schools were not, therefore, 'far and few between in the Highlands', as asserted even very recently; and there were also schools set up on local charitable bequests, those of the SSPCK itself, and those privately-organized. If we take the example of the parish of Blair Atholl in Highland Perthshire in 1755, we find there no fewer than seven schools teaching some 250 pupils: one parochial school, one SSPCK school, two schools supported by government through the Forfeited Estates Commission, and three schools in remote corners which were entirely maintained by the families who lived there.

Nor were Highland communities content only with schooling in the rudiments. There were, for example, complaints made to the SSPCK that its policy of restricting its teachers to the 3Rs was wrong-headed. A remarkable letter of 1760 is worth quoting. It was sent to the SSPCK in Edinburgh by the moderator of the presbytery of Gairloch on behalf of the inhabitants of the parish of Gairloch, asking the Society to give £10 sterling yearly, to be added to the £8 which could be raised locally, in order to establish a 'proper school' there, one with a well-educated master 'who can teach Latin or anything else they incline to their children'

> As to the objection that your schools are intended for the benefit of the poorer sort, you cannot, sir, but be sensible that the schools which are best for the children of the richer sort are likewise best for the poor. And where a school is so bad that it is not worth the richer people's while to send their children to it, the poor will reap little benefit by it. Besides that, the example of the richer sort is necessary to bring the poorer to send their children to school. We are therefore ready to join the honest people in promising to you that the children of the poor shall have full justice done to them

and make at least as good progress at such a school, as they can be supposed to do at any school in the present Establishment.

This plea, and others sent to Edinburgh, seem to have made no impact on the SSPCK, at least officially. Yet, here and there, Society teachers went well beyond the rudiments in their teaching. In the vast Upper Deeside parish of Glenmuick, Tullich and Glencairn, for instance, where the Society school changed its location every three years or so to spread the benefit of it throughout a very large area, we find a schoolteacher regularly instructing his pupils in mathematics and book-keeping, and proudly recording in his diary in 1760 that his former pupils were by then to be found in counting houses throughout the known world. To assume that only a few schools (and, at best, nearly all of these inadequate charity schools) were to be found in the eighteenth-century Highlands is seriously to misjudge the reality of their situation.

True, the devastating economic upsets of the 1770s-1790s, and the emigration of many of the 'best spirits' in local communities may well have weakened both the impulse and their ability to provide 'proper schooling' throughout the Gaidhealtachd, but neither died away. We know, for instance, from the returns to Sinclair's *Account* for the island of Skye, that all the parishes there were still remarkably well provided with schools, including grammar schools. Yet many ministers, making their returns in the 1790s, seem deliberately to have mentioned only the public schools they had, along with the major Society schools, leaving aside all account of the unendowed private schooling which was then so common: for instance, the employment for three months or longer by families in remote districts of a young man, who was boarded out in turn among them and thus transferred the school from one dwelling to another, teaching reading and perhaps writing to all their children, a teacher who returned or was replaced year by year, until all the children could read and, probably, also write and count a little.

Since the 1780s, the parochial schoolmasters had been pressing for some improvement in salaries, badly affected by inflation, and in 1803 government acted. It had two main concerns: firstly, to improve the quality of public schooling by attracting better teachers, ensuring that both improved salaries and accommodation were provided for them by their parishes; secondly, to give those parishes the right to raise by local taxation up to 600 merks a year (nearly £35 sterling) as a public fund out of which each locality could employ, in addition to the principal parochial schoolmaster, such number of 'side schools' or supplementary publicly-funded schools as seemed to be required, with lesser stipends but, as always, able to add to their modest salaries whatever fees their teachers were able to command from the parents.

While this act mainly amended and extended the existing Scottish parliament's act of 1696, it also brought profound and far-reaching effects. Not only did it bring forward a period of astonishing development in the old parochial system, reviving its fortunes (and the financial returns to its teachers), and generally improving standards, it quietly transferred important powers

An early nineteenth-century schoolroom, from A System of Education for the Young *by Samuel Wilderspin, 1840.*

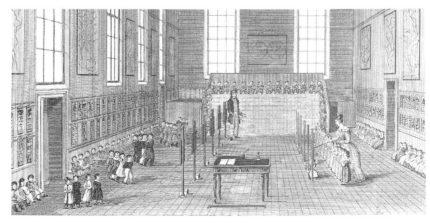

from the Church to the state. Questions about salary, matters of curriculum, problems over school accommodation, even the disciplining of teachers, were put more directly into the hands of the substantial landowners, and were referred more frequently to the county commissioners of supply (the sustantial heritors again in another guise), to local magistrates and JPs, and more and more often to the sheriffs. A quiet but important revolution in management had begun.

5 Government intervention

One leading feature, indeed, of the following thirty years and more was that parliament, increasingly through the agency of the sheriffs, began a long series of enquiries into Scottish education. It initiated extensive parish-by-parish surveys in 1818, 1826, 1834 and 1838, before in 1839 setting up a Committee on Education of the Privy Council, which for two decades became a main avenue for learning about and for increasing its control over the schooling of the masses. When legislation was at last passed in 1872, after many earlier but unsuccessful attempts to 'extend and improve' Scottish schooling, it ended one form of state intervention and began another, rather than introducing it for the first time.

The 1818 enquiry, made at a time of great concern over the social and political disruptions in the aftermath of the Napoleonic Wars, was intended to investigate the provision that existed (or did not exist) for the education of the poor in London, then was extended to the rest of England and Wales, and then to Scotland. In Scotland, the parish ministers who made the returns were generally unable to distinguish schools for the poor from others (and objected to the implication that they should or could do so); hence the Scottish replies offer a more wide-ranging and complete picture of educational provision than those for England and Wales. From the Scottish evidence a number of important conclusions can be drawn.

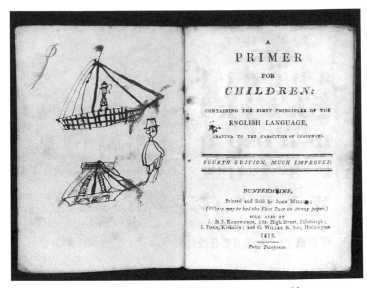

A school primer, dated 1815. A fourth edition, so presumably widely used.

Firstly, for the country as a whole, with some 1 in 9 of the population at school, Scotland came very close to the figure (1 in 8) which was then considered a very satisfactory level of provision, one that was believed to give ample opportunity for universal schooling. Central and central-west districts (7.6) and the Borders (at 8.5) were better than the average; rather surprisingly, the north-east counties – despite being known as a well-provided region – returned only 1 in 12 at school. However, this may reflect only a difference in patterns of school attendance (shorter but more continuous in the north-east, longer but more intermittent elsewhere) than anything else. Secondly, there was much variety in the amount of schooling directly provided from public funding under the 1803 Act: 60 per cent in the Borders, over 40 per cent in the north-east, Fife and the Lothians, but 35 per cent in the Highlands and only some 25 per cent in west-central Scotland. Only in this last region was more than half of all schooling (as much as 70 per cent, indeed) provided in unendowed, private adventure schools, set up 'on adventure' for the profit obtained from fees alone. Thirdly, even in the largest towns, the ministers reported that the poorer classes were 'abundantly provided with the means of education' (Aberdeen), or had 'easy access to any of the schools, either gratis or for a very small fee' (Edinburgh, Glasgow, Dundee). But the return from Gorbals, then still a suburb of Glasgow, pointed to a problem which the extent of available provision alone could not cure: 'The means of education are so ample, that where the children are not educated it must be from extreme regardlessness in themselves or gross negligence in their parents.'

And yet in the 1820s and 1830s there was much talk among the leaders of the Church of Scotland about the need for government to support the Church, through parliamentary grants, in its efforts to extend and improve schooling. In truth, however, the issue was not that there were unsurmountable barriers (even in the Highlands) which were thwarting parents' desires to obtain an education of some kind for their children, for there was schooling aplenty. What the spokesmen for the Church were keen to argue was that secure moral and religious training could only be had in the public schools, that is schools which were directly, and legally, under the supervision of the national church; yet, as we have seen, only in the Borders did they account for more than half of the available provision. The danger, in the eyes of the increasingly important Evangelical party in the Church, led by Dr Thomas Chalmers, was that very large numbers of the youth of Scotland were already, or were under threat of, being instructed by men and women outside the religious Establishment, members of dissenting churches or persons of unknown religion or even of no religion at all. Chalmers was particularly determined to renew the fortunes of the national church in the large towns, where it was losing out badly to presbyterian dissent and where the great majority of schools were outside and beyond

Church influence and oversight. For the Evangelicals the best means of renewing the community-led parochial tradition and regaining the dominance of the Church, there and elsewhere in the country, was to squeeze out the non-public schools by erecting a greatly extended national system, financially supported by the state and closely supervised by the state Church. The Church Evangelicals were not averse to claiming, mischievously, that Scotland was 'a half-educated nation' (in the title of a Church defence pamphlet in 1834), on the grounds that only half the nation's children could be accommodated in parochial schools and in others which were then under Church supervision.

The report in 1834 gave the largest attendances at school, on average in Scotland as a whole, as reaching the level of 1 in 9 of the population; best in the Lothians and Fife (7.9), worst in the west central area (10.7). However, the numbers of children aged 5-15 years who were reported as reading or learning to read were given as 1 in 5.6 of the whole population; about 1 in 12 were writing or learning to write, a proportion which may well have reflected a notable drop in the number of girls who were being instructed in this skill, especially in the Highlands and Islands. The 'tragedy' for the Church Evangelicals, however, was that only a third of all boys and a quarter of all girls were attending publicly-funded schools within the state-Church system.

Leading Liberal educational reformers in the 1820s, such as Henry Brougham, had been ready to persuade parliament to act again for Scotland, so to increase the numbers of parochial schools that they constituted a properly national system. However, they seem to have been so impressed by the evidence from the 1834 survey, so struck by the remarkable and varied response of local communities in meeting their own educational needs by adding subscription and private schools to the public provision, that they changed their minds. There was evident among these politicians a new willingness to let market-forces meet the great variety of parental demands in the country, and no longer to expect to reserve the whole of the provision to a Church-supervised state structure. (There is little doubt that this change of mind was also closely connected to the Liberals' political dependence on the votes of religious dissenters, in Scotland as well as in England.) In the end only a few so-called 'parliamentary schools' were endowed by the Treasury, in a number of huge Highland parishes.

The Church Evangelicals' response, to this clear signal of the government's determination not to react more positively to their demands, was to call on congregations to contribute to a fund to support their own Church of Scotland schools (usually called General Assembly schools) as a makeweight, until such time as the government saw the error of its ways. Paradoxically, therefore, it was the national church which edged Scotland towards giving some acceptance to sectarian provision in schooling.

In the first thirty or forty years of the nineteenth century, the provision of schooling was by no means the only centrepoint of educational discussion. The 1826 enquiry into Scottish schooling had revealed, among other things, that the public schoolmasters had generally benefited substantially from the improved stipends introduced in and after 1803; that better-qualified men were being attracted into the profession; and that their initiatives in bringing in new teaching methods and new subjects were also bringing in more fees, to the point where incomes, not infrequently, had doubled since the early years of the century. Even in distant and remote parts, the curriculum had been much expanded.

Dr J S Memes, Rector of Ayr Academy, 1825-44.

Three photographs of Kilmaurs school – before 1835, between 1835 and 1873, and after 1873 illustrate its evolution from tiny parish school to substantial public school. From Kilmaurs Parish and Burgh *by D M'Naught.*

If we look at the Highlands and Islands as a whole, for instance, and we confine our attention to the range of subjects being taught only in the parochial schools there, the 1826 returns show that over a half were regularly teaching Latin and book-keeping, a third and more offered Greek and English grammar, a quarter taught mathematics, while French, land mensuration, geography and navigation were available in a fifth of them, together with a goodly scattering of other 'higher' subjects, all these in addition to the teaching everywhere of reading in English (and often in Gaelic), writing and arithmetic. Nor was it the public schools which alone had improved, and now might teach an extended curriculum. The 1826 survey, for Lowlands and Highlands alike, shows convincingly a marked advance in the range of subjects available (and by implication in the quality of instruction) in the non-public schooling which was being provided locally by groups of parent-subscribers and by private adventurers.

In the surveys in 1834 and 1838, comment was made (and directly asked for in 1838) about the teaching styles employed by both public and private schoolteachers. Parish ministers and the masters (and mistresses) alike were keen to reveal the adoption of new monitorial systems, then much in vogue, and especially the introduction of the 'intellectual' method in their instructions: the latter, the use of question-and-answer methods, in order to ensure better attention and greater interest and understanding in the pupils, rather than depending on older forms of rote-learning and declamation, was very widely reported. Greater attentiveness to the moral education of the youth was stressed, with a widely-voiced demand that the benefits of infant schooling should be promoted everywhere and that all intending teachers should have a period of training and so improve the quality of their instruction. At much the same time, too, there was rising pressure for the wider use of assistant teachers (perhaps along with, but mostly in preference to, monitors) in order to overcome the management problems which could face a single-handed master struggling to cope with a very heterogeneous array of 40 or 60 or 80 pupils of all ages, and at all stages, in one room.

One writer, looking back from 1851 to his own schooldays 'fifty years since', recalled what had been a typical schoolroom at the turn of the century:

What a chaos of confusion! Division of labour had then scarcely dawned; classification was in its rudest state. High over the hoarse murmur of unsuppressed idlers, the few who were actively engaged with the master screamed out their recital. . . Next the door, on rude and low forms, sat the younger branches, confined for four hours a day, perhaps superintended by some of the older pupils. . . Behind these there was a helper who superintended a class in reading the Old Testament. . . In another quarter, at tables, sat the arithmeticians or 'counters', some mumbling over the multiplication table and wondering why all the lines were not so easy as the tenth. . . Beyond that sat, in more dignified position and seclusion, the Latin scholars, each flanked by a dictionary sheathed in old writing copies. . . Not far off sat a few mathematicians, who were regarded by the other pupils with an air of reverence, as a kind of magicians, while they wielded their scales and

An interpretation of High School Yards, Edinburgh, as they were in the early nineteenth century, painted by Le Conte in 1874.

Going to school in Lochaber, by R R MacIan, from Highlanders at Home, *1848. The 'horn laddie' blew the horn to attract the attention of other children who had to undertake what was often a long walk to school.*

School at Glenquoich in Inverness-shire, K J Ellice, 1847

Examination of Doon school by the Presbytery, by Jemima Blackburn,
1823-1909. The teacher is Miss Gibson, the examiner Mr Gordon
of Twynholm.

The Village School *by Sir George Harvey, 1806-76.*

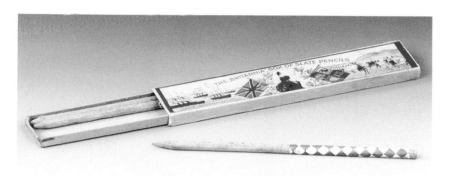

Slate pencils and box, nineteenth century.

The Visit of
the Patron and
Patroness to the
Village School *by
Thomas Faed, 1851.*

*School girls depicted
in* Intermission *by
James Cowie, 1935.*

compasses. Besides them, unmindful of their occasional frays, would sit some thoughtful lad who, in consequence of an in-come or injury to his leg, had been advised to turn his mind to learning, and who was now engaged in balancing a set of book-keeping by double-entry. . .

As school numbers increased in the early decades of the century, masters were driven to move from the informal use of older boys and girls to help their younger companions (such as we saw in the seventeenth-century school rules) to more structured monitorial systems – perhaps those advertised and paraded by Dr Bell (a Scot who, initiating his scheme of working in India, called it the Madras system) or by Joseph Lancaster from England, these being applicable to very large schools indeed. In England, these systems, formally adopted by both Anglicans and Dissenters, were very widely employed and proved effective enough in teaching the unlettered the rudiments and other elementary skills. In larger schools in Scotland, in towns and also in populous country areas, whose curricula incorporated a wide range of the more advanced subjects, 'Bell' and 'Lancasterian' methodologies were much more sparingly used. When arrangements were made to introduce assistant masters and mistresses, in order to cope with the sheer pressure of numbers in Scottish schools which provided an extended curriculum, then it was that 'classification' (or the division of the pupils into distinct classes) began, in its stuttering way, to appear. But before these developments, in a 'numerous' parochial school without the benefit of an usher or assistant master, as our commentator recalled in 1851, the schoolmaster's day could be a fraught one:

All these advanced pupils prepared their lesson during the day, while the master went through the multifarious duties of the more ignoble classes which, one by one, were drawn up successively to the middle of the floor where, forming a ring, they rehearsed their lessons. The general hum, or rather continuous roar, of the whole school rendered it necessary that every boy in the ring should, in order to be audible to the master, stretch his lungs to the utmost extent, the vehemence of the recital dilating each eye and contracting each forehead. Around them incessantly flitted the dominie, whose attention was distracted by the hosts of enquiries on all sides from the various regions of learning. . .one of the younger fraternity whining for leave to go out, an arithmetician whose count defeated him, an emissary from the classical department to report that a word was not to be found in the dictionary. . .

Educational debates included, too, a review of the forms of discipline used in schools. What could ensure something more than a mere semblance of order in the schoolroom and thus could allow a more fruitful learning to take place? It was no real surprise that in the elaborate questionnaire which government addressed to all teachers (parochial and non-parochial) in 1838, there were requests for information not only about teaching methods but also about how they enforced discipline. The answers clearly implied that the 'intellectual system' had improved both learning and control, and there was an impressive consensus about the value of avoiding too ready a use of corporal punishment. While it is difficult to judge how just or true a picture is conveyed by these public statements, our commentator in 1851, in his reminiscing about conditions fifty years earlier, was keen to stress the beneficial changes that had taken place in school discipline. In his view, 'many of the improvements of modern education have sprung from the increasing civilization and humanities of later times':

That severity of discipline, for instance, which reigned so long in many of our seminaries was but a counterpart of the co-existent harshness of domestic rule. The rod was the short way to order in families as in schools – the taws in Scotland was a necessary part of the nursery furniture. . . Some parents, indeed, were unreasonable enough to recommend to the master a different course, and to insist on a system of persuasion and conciliation which was not adopted in their own families should be attempted at school; but this selfish demand imposed a task which few could have accomplished. The teacher acted according to the spirit of the age, and when we consider the great numbers which, in common schools, were often committed to his charge; the want of classification which was then almost necessary from the irregular attendance of the pupils; the absence of many of those higher branches which give variety and interest to a school course; the entire want of sympathy on the part of the parent, and the consequent want of respect on behalf of the pupil – who can wonder that the teacher then was 'a man severe and stern to view'. . .

Lack of support from certain recalcitrant parents was, however, still a problem at mid-century. In fact, teachers were said to look in vain for what had been once seen as the expected and traditional support of their pupils' families; some (still relatively few?) parents were cavalier and careless about securing their children's attendance at school and withdrew them too early in order to put them to work. Intermittently, but increasingly, the state was pressed to do what once the local church had done, to ensure that parents put their children regularly to school.

6 The Disruption and the fight for national education

Whenever governments had confronted the challenge of improving Scottish education in the earlier nineteenth century, they assumed that it should be based on extending the parochial school system as established by law in 1696 and 1803. But, as we have seen, the succession of surveys from 1818 to 1838 had gone far to convince them that what had 'naturally' grown up, the existing mixture of state, charitable, community-funded and private schooling, was well able to supply the demand for school places, even in Lowland industrial areas into which additional population was flooding. One considerable advantage in Scotland was that both public and private schooling was, by and large, non-denominational. Formal religious teaching was generally confined to the reading of the Bible and the learning of the presbyterian Shorter Catechism, something acceptable to or demanded by the bulk of the people; Episcopalian and Roman Catholic pupils, and any others, could be excused from either or both at their parents' request. Some schools, however, in areas with very mixed populations, seem to have offered to teach a variety of catechetical statements, on demand. The sectarian divisions in the adult population, presbyterian or other, were not then mirrored in Scottish schooling.

The situation in England, much troubled by fierce disputes between Anglicans and Dissenters of all kinds, was quite different. These two groupings had long vied with each other in promoting distinctive systems of elementary schools, and since 1820 had done so with the aid of modest government grants. In 1839, government established a Committee of the Privy Council on Education to regulate and oversee these grants, with the help of an appointed inspectorate. In the beginning the new system was not meant to be applied in Scotland, but it soon spread north.

During the 1830s Church (or the Church Evangelicals who controlled the General Assembly after 1834) and state confronted each other over two main points: the rights of laymen to exercise patronage in Church appointments, nominating candidates for the filling of vacancies in the parish ministry; and the refusal of the state to give financial support for the building of new Established churches and new schools in urban and other areas of fast-rising population. In 1843, at the Disruption, one third of all the ministers and about half the members left the Church of Scotland and formed the Free Church. Almost at once, nearly 80 parochial schoolmasters, members of the new church, resigned or were dismissed from their schools. The rallying cry went up, in the first great wave of enthusiasm, that in order to accommodate these teachers, but also to confirm the new church's standing as the 'true' church of the nation, Free Church schools should be provided for all the Free Church people. By 1851 the Free Church Education Committee was recorded as supporting, in one way or another, some 600-700 schools, adding substantially to the numbers of school places, especially where the new church was strong in the Highlands and Islands and in many Lowland urban areas.

Yet perhaps as many as one half of all these Free Church schools were not new foundations but were existing subscription and adventure schools which had been transferred into the new church. And when the 1851 religious census was published, including its survey of schooling, it would show that only 17 per cent of all Scottish pupils attended Free Church schools: a very remarkable achievement no doubt, but not the alternative national system which had been hoped for. There were then still 25 per cent of all scholars within the parochial system; and in

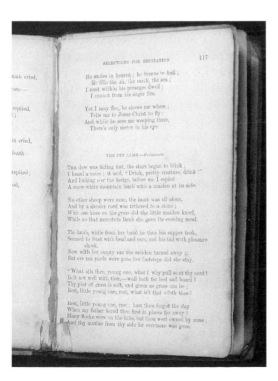

Selections for Recitation, *a typical nineteenth-century school book.*

addition another 17 per cent in schools which were also directly connected with the Church of Scotland as a sect – Assembly, SSPCK, congregational and sessional schools. Yet, the most significant finding was that 44 per cent of all schools, containing 34 per cent of all pupils, had no formal religious or sectarian attachment whatsoever, and these were mainly subscription and private adventure schools. Neither the parochial and burgh schools, nor those provided by all the churches put together, can be said to have dominated provision in Scotland.

Some time before these results were published, the Disruption had made another kind of impact on Scottish schooling. The early fervour and enthusiasm of the Free Church had greatly outrun its resources, and by 1846 its education scheme was in very severe financial difficulties. And this at a time when tales abounded that the children of the poorest classes in the towns were being left unschooled (although not always because there were no school places available). A group within the old Free Church leadership argued that the presbyterian churches in Scotland should unite to press government to incorporate all existing schools, sectarian and other, into an inclusive national system and add new 'national' schools wherever these were needed. The new structure was to be provided for by local taxation and put under local management committees properly representative of all taxpayers, with suitable measures taken to ensure the attendance of those of school age.

This move was heavily defeated in the Free Church Assembly, in favour of saving and extending their own scheme by accepting grants-in-aid for building schools and topping up teachers' stipends which the Committee of Council was to make available to any religious sect. It was objected, firstly, that it was demeaning for the Free Church to bid for government favours on

A child reading under the benign gaze of grandparents, suggesting the value that was placed on children learning to read. Walter Geikie (1795-1837)

a par with an error-laden, detested and idolatrous Roman Catholicism (soon to be able for the first time to apply for grants) and, secondly, that the new grants would only strengthen sectarianism in Scotland and would seriously weaken the chances of persuading government to legislate for an extended and truly national system of schools. This latter warning, glibly turned aside by the younger Free Church leadership, would prove all too correct. Successive attempts in parliament in the later 1840s and throughout the 1850s to establish a new, national and inclusive educational system did fail, and failed mainly because of heightened sectarian rivalries exacerbated by the Committee of Council grants policy. Furthermore, grants for the maintenance of separate Church and Free Church teacher-training colleges (normal schools) in Glasgow and Edinburgh, underlined a new, sharpening divide in Scottish education.

And yet it would be wrong to overplay the importance of direct state aid in Scotland, in comparison with its huge significance in supporting the provision for elementary or popular schooling in England. South of the Border over 40 per cent of all expenditure came from Privy Council grants, 34 per cent was contributed by the various churches, and 20 per cent came locally from fees. In Scotland, however, direct state aid accounted in 1864 for only 15 per cent of all funding for schools, while the churches together provided only 10 per cent. Remarkably, some 74 per cent of all expenditure was raised locally: 21 per cent by law from the heritors and tenants, 33 per cent from fees, and 20 per cent from subscriptions and gifts. The Scottish system was still, in essence and crucially, community-led and community-funded.

7 Interference from the centre

Bewilderingly, the Committee of Council still treated both countries as if there were no essential differences in the character of, or the idealisms which underlay, two very different modes of providing schools for the people. For twenty years after 1847 complaint after complaint was levelled against the effects of the Privy Council system. For one thing, despite the Committee's insistence that its prime function was to extend opportunities for schooling for the poor in areas of scanty provision, the Privy Council's regulations had left unhelped too many areas of need. The demand that half of the costs, of building for instance, had to be raised locally before any aid could be given, meant that in Scotland (where localities were already so heavily committed in school funding) the poorest areas of the Highlands and of the urban Lowlands were too often ignored. Yet the Council was ready to make grants-in-aid to Assembly and Free Church schools, within a stone's throw of each other, where one would clearly have been sufficient. Long before its misguided and unsuccessful attempt to impose a new set of regulations (the Revised Code) on Scottish schools in the early 1860s, the Committee of Council was under attack for what were seen as its ignorant English ways. For instance, in 1853, its secretary – Sir James Kay-Shuttleworth,

Gayfield Square School for Girls, Edinburgh, in 1865 – a very early photograph of a school class in Scoltand. This was a school for blind girls. SLA

as he would become – published a book entitled *Public Education* in which the Council's usual attack on so-called dames' schools and private adventure schools in England and Wales was extended, carelessly, to Scotland. A teacher-reviewer offered this rejoinder:

> There are certain statements concerning the present state of education in Scotland which at once we beg respectfully to characterize as undistinguishing and unguarded. The great majority of adventure schools in Scotland are denounced as an opprobrium to civilization. One-third of the children who ought to be at school in Scotland receive no public instruction; and one half of the remainder are so taught by incompetent masters that their education is almost fruitless.' We cannot admit the truth of these statements.

> As regards the adventure schools, many of them in towns have been superseded by subscription and sessional schools, but this circumstance does not mean that the adventure schools were ill-conducted – indeed, many of their teachers have been employed in the new establishments. Numbers of these schools still exist in the principal towns of Scotland, and these frequently are the most respectable and thoroughly taught schools; in many of the larger villages they are also to be found. . . It may be said that the offensive remarks had reference only to elementary schools in obscure parishes; but in a work professing to give a fair estimate of the condition of education in Scotland, the ignoring of the existence of a large body of men by whose means, especially in large towns, a great part of the higher and middle classes are taught, is extremely unfair. . . The creation of many subscription schools, whose working is conducted by active and intelligent committees, the establishment of sessional schools in towns, and the increased watchfulness exercised by heritors and clergymen in the appointment of parochial teachers, have all tended to render the situation of the adventure teacher a hopeless one, provided he is not well accomplished, active and enthusiastic. . . but the education which is now given in our towns, and Lowland parishes and villages, is in a great proportion of cases throughly useful and practical. It is

certainly superior to that of many years ago, when Scotch education was as much lauded in England as it is now decried. The dame schools –which still form a considerable part of the English system of education –have long since disappeared in Scotland, and comparatively few Scotchmen or Scotchwomen are reduced to 'his or her mark' – a notation characteristic of the Southron. . .

This is only one of a legion of complaints about the Council's almost wilful disregard for the distinctiveness of Scottish schooling, which reached a crescendo in the early 1860s. These were to be paraded before another government enquiry, a royal commission under the Duke of Argyll which sat from 1864 until 1868, issuing a series of weighty and detailed reports, the results of extensive statistical surveys, and recommendations which included a draft bill. Already, even before the Commission had been set up in 1864, the census of 1861 had included returns about school attendance; but the commissioners decided to add their own enquiry to this, to be carried out by local registrars. Both surveys confirmed that enrolments of children (aged 5-14 years, inclusive) were very high: 1 in 6.5 of the whole population over the whole country, and even 1 in 6.6 in the Inner and Outer Hebrides. The registrars also noted actual attendances at the times of their enquiries: 1 in 8 or 1 in 9 were generally to be found at school. A special survey made a little later of the inner city districts of Glasgow, assumed to be the worst in Scotland, revealed that 1 in 8.9 of the population there were enrolled, and in attendance at some time, in either day or evening schools.

These returns, remarkably good in European terms, did not support the partisan comments of some churchmen that very serious deficiences in school provision existed in the largest towns and in the Highlands. More than that, direct questioning in the localities about whether additional schools were needed produced surprisingly few demands for new ones, and even these were frequently suggested for the sake of convenience rather than out of necessity. Thus, provision was perhaps not the major issue.

Kingsford School, Stewarton, Ayrshire, in 1863.

The commissioners then turned their attention to the 'effectiveness' of existing schooling; but again the evidence from witnesses and other data was to bring little cause for concern, if effectiveness was judged in terms of the general ability of the population at large to read, to write, and to demonstrate a basic numeracy. There were undoubted blackspots: the education of the children of the poor Catholic Irish in Glasgow was one, but even there it was poor attendance and too short a period of schooling which seemed to be the main troubles. The commissioners turned next to what proved to be much safer ground for them. Were the organization and management of schooling in Scotland 'efficient'?

Here at least the answers could be determined (and definitions agreed) by the Commission itself and its expert advisers, the government-appointed inspectorate. Government interests quickly came to the fore. Was the nation getting value for the money it expended on schooling, from public and from other sources? What. in the name of efficiency, ought to be demanded of managers, of teachers, of parents, and of children themselves?

The Commissioners wrote, rather despairingly, of the 'confusion of agencies' which supported schooling in Scotland, and implied that there was a recognized need for the imposition of a simpler and more coherent structure, one under more effective direction. But we should ask for whom, and in what, that supposed confusion lay. Neither in the Commission's evidence, nor in the newspapers or journals of the day, is there much sign that the customers of the existing structure, parents or children, were 'confused'. In fact, the complex and often highly-differentiated provision of schools had itself been shaped by customer demand; it reflected, whether publicly or privately supported, the changing numbers, the geographical spread, the career intentions, and the fee-paying potential of would-be pupils. In many towns, and in populous and close-knit parishes, it was not unusual for pupils to attend not one school for the whole day but two or even three schools for parts of the day, for different subjects of instruction. The teaching day was not heavily regulated: for some masters and mistresses it might stretch from 6.30 in the morning until 9.30 in the evening, in order to accommodate different groups. The curricula offered, the sizes of available schools, their scales of fees, the character and professional capabilities of their teachers, the social environment of the schools and the clienteles they attracted, all these gave grounds for choice. True that choice could be limited – by what was available in a particular district, by the ability to pay, etc – but neither the choice nor its limitations could be said to be 'confusing' to the customers. Whether this varied provision, driven by market forces, was equitable for all groups in society, was altogether another issue; but it was not perplexing to those who had grown up with it.

The driving force in the Commission's deliberations was, without doubt, the government's concern to regulate and to reduce public expenditure: for that a simplified, more easily-controlled and centrally-directed structure of schooling was desirable. And it seemed to be attainable in Scotland in the later 1860s. The presbyterian churches were all finding the support of

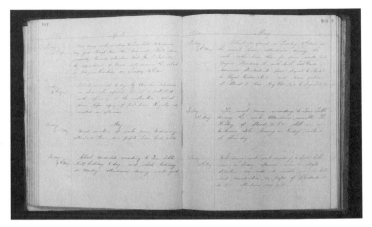

Pages for April and May 1884 from the log book of Ruskie School in Perthshire, kept from 1873 to 1906. On 17 April the school was examined by the minister. Attendance – 'variable', 'good', 'very good' – and holidays are recorded. The week's work – 'school conducted according to timetable' – is noted.

their own schools a severe drain on resources, just when they were all anxious about the apparent decline in membership and attachment to them among the adult population. Compulsory schooling in a new national system, providing a firm but modest instruction in (presbyterian) Christian values to the next generation, seemed an appealing prospect. And in Scotland, the Episcopalians and Roman Catholics were too small in numbers to be bothersome. One Free Church minister saw national schooling as the only sure way to combat, long-term, the rising tide of non-church-going:

> The young are so early put to labour, and become so soon independent of their parents, and are so constantly encompassed by endless temptations and means of indulgence, and at the same time parents themselves are generally so unable to discipline their children, that the only likelihood of having them reared in Christian knowledge is to provide it in the daily schools of instruction.

8 The democratic tradition

One of the witnesses to the Argyll Commission remarked that, in contrast with English practice, it was the state's task, within the Scottish tradition, 'to overtake the education of the people' and not merely 'to effect the education of a class'. Here he was joining in a well-rehearsed attack on the Privy Council's policies: that it had too often refused government aid to the most needy places and that it had been notoriously weak in supporting the teaching of subjects beyond the 3Rs; worse still, recently the Council had demanded that, since its grants were meant only to support teaching for the poorest classes, each aided school had to report

Glencoe village school, Argyll, in about 1900, but probably unchanged for at least a century. Slots at the front of the benches hold the children's slates. SLA

on the social background of all its pupils' parents. And, rather than follow out the last demand, school after school was preparing to withdraw from the Committee of Council scheme: Scottish schools were open to all in their communities; hence the instruction was offensive and alien to the Scottish tradition. The Argyll Commission found itself struggling, throughout its proceedings, to balance the public's insistence on maintaining the best of Scottish tradition against the narrow definitions of 'value for money' and the class-conscious pronouncements of the Lords of Council.

The weakening of the Scottish tradition had also come under earlier scrutiny. In 1858, for example, writing in *The People's Journal*, a schoolmaster from Johnshaven in Kincardineshire, W D Latto, remarked that a poor country lad would at school gain only 'a smatterin' acquaintance wi' readin', wreatin', and arithmetic –the three simples, whilk, when mixed in certain due proportions, are popularly believed to be sufficient to form that important compound commonly ca'd education'. And then, at the age of eight or nine, this same lad – 'nae mair than half edicated' – would be sent out in the world to earn a living. The poor wages allowed by farmers to their labourers accounted for parents' 'carelessness' in failing to provide a proper schooling to their children; and avaricious and uncaring employers, in town

This building, photographed in the 1970s, was once the schoolhouse at Rogart, Sutherland.
SLA

and in country alike, with a selfish concern only for profit, vied with each other to take on cheap workers at much too early an age. So limited had become the instruction recently offered to, and able to be enjoyed by, the labourer's son or daughter that later self-instruction, so traditional a feature in the lives of poor-born Scots, was perforce 'neither a pleasant nor a profitable operation'. Worthy and able youths were thus too often trapped into a life bereft of honest ambition. In short, there was no value for money, for the individual or for society, in the miserably shortened education the young were receiving.

Witnesses to the Argyll Commission, and countless articles in the press, stung by the socially-divisive policies of the Committee of Council, stressed the inheritance of the Book of Discipline of 1560. Biography after biography of leading figures in Scotland (especially the ministers of the presbyterian churches) confirmed for the public the importance of maintaining access for the able poor to a schooling in the higher subjects; again and again it was noted that in Scotland these were not the preserve of the middle and upper classes, nor was access to the universities. Thus, the son of a small farmer in Pitsligo in Aberdeenshire, James Robertson, who had learned the alphabet from his mother and also at home had 'received lessons from the wife of his father's ploughman' (and that should be noted), attended two small parochial schools before going to Marischal College and University in New Aberdeen, eventually becoming professor of Ecclesiastical History at Edinburgh University. Again, there was Donald Stuart from Upper Glenlyon, his first school in a croft house there, who was sent to be a herd on a farm in Strathearn 'to learn the English that was spoken in the Perthshire Lowlands' before attending the parish school of Kenmore; at fifteen he then went to Fife, bought out the goodwill of an adventure school in Leven, and 'taught the branches of useful education' in day and evening classes; in 1840, at the age still of only 20, helped by a bursary he won in addition to his savings, he entered St Andrews University; a dozen years later, Stuart was a very prominent Free

Church minister in Dunedin, New Zealand. Such success stories abounded: a good parochial school was, for those who wanted to make full use of it, a revered highway to a better life for the poor man's son, as a Brechin pedlar's poem of the mid-nineteenth century underlined:

> Wha kens but ye may get a school, An' syne ye'll win our bread?
> Wha kens but in a pu'pit yet, We'll see you wag your head?
> Our minister an' dominie were laddies in their day,
> An' like you had to learn at e'en, the A, B, C.

Indeed, one report to the Argyll Commission gave particular attention to the social profile of the Scottish universities. Of their first-year students in 1865-66, some 30 per cent came from the professional classes, and 20 per cent had fathers who were in commerce, in a large or a small way; 18 per cent were 'agricultural' in family origin, the sons of proprietors or tenants of all kinds; remarkably, no fewer than 20 per cent were the sons of artisans, and skilled or unskilled labourers. (The social backgrounds of the remaining 12 per cent were unknown.)

Thus, the 'lad o pairts' was still in evidence in Scotland. Yet even the most adamant supporters of improved access to higher education for the able poor had no expectation that there could or even should be equal opportunity for access for them and the higher social orders. Even the *Book of Discipline* had recognized that. The democratic tradition lay in access being available, in its not being denied merely because of social background, not (as has been sometimes assumed) in any cast-iron assurance that in all circumstances the opportunity for advanced studies could be as readily taken up by the poor as it could by the rich. What was

Silver medal awarded for Greek at Montrose Academy, 1882.

looked for from the Argyll commissioners in the late 1860s was that they should try to revitalize and restore what was most valuable in the distinctiveness of Scottish schooling and constrain Council influence where it was running counter to Scottish sensitivities. Yet they remained remarkably hesitant in the proposals they made in their draft bill, perhaps because it was not quite so self-evident as sometimes suggested that the existing system was in fact failing the country.

9 The Education (Scotland) Act, 1872

Two unsuccessful bills, closely based on the Argyll draft, preceded a much more radical measure in 1872. This gave no quarter to the non-parochial and private schools: these could be transferred into the new national system, under local elected school

Alexander's Public School, run by the Glasgow School Board. Typical of the more formidable buildings put up after the 1872 Education Act.

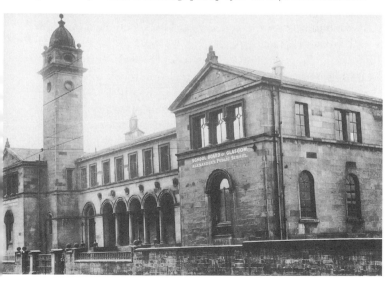

boards, or be left outside to survive on their own without rate-aid. And it was mainly the Episcopalian and Roman Catholic schools which held out. By 1878 only 669 schools out of a total of 3011, and after 1914 only 343 out of 3371, remained outside school board management: in 1918 the remaining church schools were incorporated into the national system. State schooling was thus made dominant in Scotland, unlike in England where a 'dual system' had given the advantage to the voluntary schools, leaving the school boards with only a remnant of the school population – with the poorest, with 'those with little to know and little to pay'. There would be no social stigma in Scotland for the vast majority of the people to be taught together within the state system. And the national schools in Scotland, as the Act intended or so it seemed, were not – as in England – to be restricted to the teaching of the elements.

Only at the last gasp was a clause introduced into the 1872 Act which admitted any formal religious instruction into the board schools, according to 'use and wont', with parents having the right of withdrawal. A Board of Education in Edinburgh, but only a temporary one, was set up to oversee and regulate the new system. And parents were to be required to send their children to school until they reached either a modest standard of accomplishment or the age of thirteen. A new committee of the Privy Council to be called the Scotch Education Department (SED) was set up, with its own inspectorate: it soon developed extensive managerial powers, over school boards as well as the schoolteachers; and in 1885 would be released from its connection with the Privy Council when, while still located in London, it was put under the looser control of the new Secretaryship of State for Scotland.

The 1872 Act not only marked a striking change in educational administration, it introduced something close to a new culture of schooling. Looking back in 1920, one writer recalled that 'after the Education Act of 1872, under the direction of cast-iron codes, the annual inspection developed into an organized series

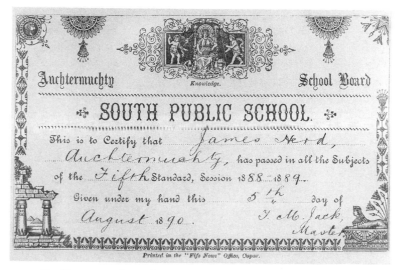

Certificate awarded to James Herd, who `passed in all the Subjects of the Fifth Standard' at South Public School, Auchtermuchty, 1890. SLA

of terrors. . . Any flaw was visited by the most terrible of punishments – a loss of grant. Every pass or failure could be computed in terms of L.s.d.' The iron rule of the inspectors, mirrored in the painstaking efforts of teachers to meet their every requirement, too often transferred a dull and humourless rigidity to the classroom. The SED, with its codes and circulars, under the direction of successive and domineering permanent secretaries, took an astonishingly tight control over Scottish schooling. In the major towns, the school boards, often a battleground not only for sectarian and political animosities but also between the spenders and those who strained to contain or reduce rates, were always ready to maximize monies available from central funds by following out SED policies. Hence, women teachers, cheaper to employ, joined the staffs of the state schools in unprecedented numbers. And in the cities there appeared very large schools, perhaps to accommodate 800 or even 1000, another enormous change since 1872 in the school experience of pupils; generally, they were now confined in separate classrooms with those of the same age, imprisoned (as it sometimes seemed) in gaunt, dark barracks, and frequently restrained there by military-style discipline. A north-east poet, J C Milne, sensed the new flavour in town schooling:

> As I gaed doon by kirk and toon,
> Quo I, "A skweel, gweed feth!"
> And there I heard nae sang nor soun',
> But bairns quaet as death!

Later, with more irony, he reflected on the impact of the new system on country teachers and pupils (after 1918 there were also county directors of education):

> Fae Monday morn till Friday nicht I'd yark the learnin in
> Though I widna touch the fancy frills, for that wid be a sin!
> Nae drawin, singin, dancin – they're the cantrips o' the Deil!
> Na, I widna hae sik ongauns in my couthy country skweel.
>
> But O the reams o writin a' my littlins aye wid dae!
> And siccan lists o spellin's ilka nicht they'd learn for me!
> And dyod the aul' Director wid dance a highland reel
> Gin he cam, but that's nae likely, te my couthy country skweel.

A policy of compulsory attendance was introduced in 1872 and confirmed in 1878. It was characteristic that, when the Treasury released funds in 1889 and 1891 for educational purposes, whereas in England (where board schools were virtually confined to the lower classes) these were mainly used to reduce rates, in Scotland they were used to reduce or abolish school fees and to develop advanced or 'secondary' subjects in the national schools. Lack of proper funding or support by the SED for such advanced schooling had long been attacked as a pernicious denial of opportunity for access to higher studies.

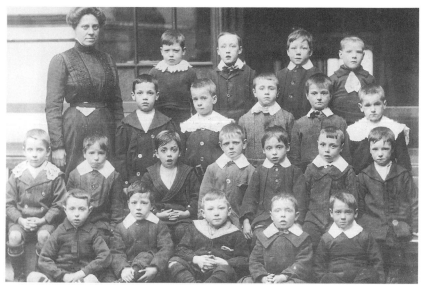

St James Public School, Calton, Glasgow, in 1911.

10 Secondary schooling for all ?

Perhaps the most unrelenting debate for fifty years and more after 1872 had been over advanced or secondary schooling. Despite the apparent intention of the 1872 Act, the SED had strained to enforce a clear division between one group of schools (thirteen of these in the largest towns) and the rest. The thirteen, called Higher Class Public Schools, which were thought to approximate to the middle-class grammar schools of England, were excused from the need to work within the Department's codes, were to be free from government inspection and also from the requirement to employ only teachers holding government training certificates; but they were not to be allowed any rate-aid from the local board and had to support themselves from fees. There was enormous pressure on the ordinary schools (which included the old

DIRLETON SCHOOL BOARD.

Opening of New School.

· NEW SCHOOL AT DIRLETON ·
Opened on Sept. 16th 1912 by Sir Andrew H. L. Fraser, K.C.S.I., LL.D.

PARAPHRASE XI.   Proverbs, iii. 13—17.

O happy is the man who hears
Instruction's warning voice;
And who celestial Wisdom makes
His early, only choice.
For she has treasures greater far
Than east or west unfold;
And her rewards more precious are
Than all their stores of gold.

In her right hand she holds to view
A length of happy days;
Riches, with splendid honours join'd,
Are what her left displays.
She guides the young with innocence,
In pleasure's paths to tread,
A crown of glory she bestows
Upon the hoary head.

According as her labours rise,
So her rewards increase;
Her ways are ways of pleasantness,
And all her paths are peace.

DEDICATION PRAYER—Rev. JAMES GRACIE, B.D.

Introductory Remarks by Chairman of the Board,   Rev. JOHN KERR, M.A.

ADDRESS
BY
Sir ANDREW H. L. FRASER, K.C.S.I., LL.D.

VOTE OF THANKS AND PRESENTATION OF KEY.
W. S. CURR, Esq., Ninewar.

SONG	- - - - -	"The Maple Leaf."
HIGHLAND AIR -	-	"Ho, Ro, My Nut-brown Maid."
RECITATION	- - - - -	"Visitors."

SCOTCH REEL.

ADDRESS   -   ANDREW E. SCOUGAL, Esq., LL.D.
Formerly H.M. Chief Inspector of Schools.

BENEDICTION—Rev. JAMES COULLIE, B.D.

GOD SAVE THE KING!

*Announcement of the opening of Dirleton School, September 1912.
The opening of a new school was often a matter of some pomp and
circumstance, making public the pride of the locality in what had
been achieved.* SLA

parochials) to concentrate on the teaching of the elements and reduce the time and effort spent on the higher subjects: little wonder that there were complaints that advanced or secondary schooling had been 'left to starve'. A furious and prolonged battle ensued, to try to force the SED to alter its policy. Commission after commission supported the traditionalists' view: in 1881 one stated that 'not only is it possible to combine thorough elementary teaching with instruction in the higher branches but any separation is detrimental to the tone of the school and is dispiriting to the master'. Nonetheless, the SED stuck to its policies; and, despite the codes, school after school in the country districts struggled to maintain its advanced teaching. Paradoxically, the public confrontation with the SED did much to revive awareness of the old Scottish ideals, and to decry the SED actions as anglicization.

An art class at Portobello High School, 1914. SLA

When the Department in 1888 engineered the removal, from the grasp of 'uncontrollable' universities, of the regional examinations which had grown up to mark the end of pre-university schooling, and then introduced its own national Leaving Certificate examinations, it at once restricted entry to them to the Higher Class Public Schools. Four years of uproar passed before the SED relented, and the Certificate was opened to all board schools. Ten years later, to the chagrin of the SED, some 70 per cent of all Leaving Certificate candidates were from schools other than those designated Higher Class or Higher Grade (the latter a new designation for schools prompted to specialize in science and commerce).

Not that the SED was beaten off. Once the school leaving age was raised to fourteen in 1901, it acted to introduce a new and sharp distinction at the age of twelve, between post-elementary and 'secondary' schooling: supplementary courses, under the elementary school code, for those expected to leave school at fourteen, or a five-year academic course in a secondary school. That sparked off another running battle with the SED, to keep alive the old mixed system; in 1919 it flared up again when, as part of reconstruction at the end of World War I, it was decided to raise the school leaving age to fifteen (even though this was delayed, because of the country's financial difficulties, until 1939, and then again until after World War II): and, as a result, in 1921 the SED issued new proposals for post-12 schooling in Circular 44.

This planned an 'entirely separate organization' of schooling for academic (ie would-be Higher Leaving Certificate) pupils and those expected to leave at the statutory age. There was to be no common schooling in the early post-primary years, 'even in subjects which are common to secondary and non-secondary pupils'. Only schools offering full five-year Certificate courses would be designated secondary. Even in parts of the country where the population required only one school for all post-12 pupils, cross-group teaching was to be disavowed. The declared

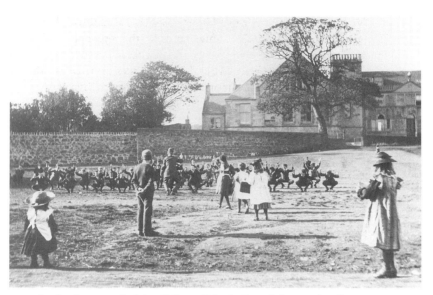

In the playground of Argyll Street School, Campbeltown, Argyll, around 1900. SLA

motivation for these changes, laudable enough in itself – 'to gain for the non-secondary pupil the full share of attention to which he is entitled' – failed to turn aside the wrath of political parties, teachers' organizations, newspapers and journals, even the government's own and independent Advisory Council on Education. The circular was condemned for its anglicizing attack on honourable traditions, for closing off access to the higher subjects, particularly to lower-class children and late developers, and for destroying social cohesion in rural areas where 'community' was still a recognizable entity. In a new and very inflexible educational world, it was complained, parents would be forced to make unnecessary and unfortunate decisions for their children when they were as young as twelve.

The opposition groups offered an alternative which would preserve opportunity, flexibility and the meritocratic tradition. They

*Dinner time at North Canongate School, Edinburgh, about 1914.
The 1908 Education Act supported the provision of meals at school,
part of an effort to improve public health.* SLA

wanted to construct a new end-on system. Common schooling at
the primary stage would be followed by three years of common
secondary schooling, topped off by an Intermediate examination
which would function as a leaving certificate for those who then
left school, and as a qualifying examination for free places in the
post-15 years which led on to the Higher Leaving Certificate (others
would still be admitted, but as fee-payers). Amazingly, no quarter
was given by the SED, and its scheme was introduced. Yet large
numbers of parents claimed places in the five-year schools – and
not only for the social cachet – even although there was every
likelihood of their children being removed at fifteen. In the mid-
1930s over a half of all post-primary pupils under the leaving
age were in Leaving Certificate courses in well-equipped and
well-staffed schools, while the SED reluctantly admitted that the

The infant room at Aberdour School in Fife, about 1933. SLA

other post-12 schools, regulated under the elementary school codes, had inferior buildings, inferior equipment, larger class numbers, and 'differently qualified' teachers. As little more than a sop to renewed criticisms, the SED renamed the latter schools and courses 'Junior Secondary', while the existing five-year schools became 'Senior Secondaries'.

By the 1940s and 1950s secondary or high schools based in country towns were generally 'omnibus' in organization – that is, they contained senior and junior secondary pupils within one set of buildings, all of them belonging to the same named institution. There might be strict academic and non-academic divides, and little interchange between classes, but (to outsiders at least) they were identified as participants in the same school community. In the largest towns, however, where there was usually an almost total separation of senior and junior secondaries, based in quite different buildings on quite different sites, there were levels of social inequality which, it has been said, often exceeded the class divisiveness which notoriously existed in England between the grammar schools and secondary modern schools of the post-1944 era.

In a book of reminiscences of Scottish education in the 1940s, *Jock Tamson's Bairns*, it is the variety of experience which comes through most strongly: all seemed to depend on just where it was that you went to school. At one primary school in Edinburgh, 'the whole point of education there was to keep us firmly in our places – to "teach" us to be completely subservient to the staff. . . The sounds I most remember from that school are the deadening sounds of Souza tunes we kids had to march upstairs to, and the sound of children being hammered in the hands of twisted adults. . .' In Skye, however, another contributor writes, 'our education was humane, uneventful and unexciting. . . We scratched on slates, graduated to copybooks, and were occasionally allowed the frivolity of plasticine. Each morning we recited psalms or learned the Shorter Catechism by rote, chanted arithmetical tables, and erupted into the playground, scrabbling

Primary One at Biggar Primary School, 1950s. It seems to be a singing class. SLA

for our shinty sticks piled in the corner of the room as we went. . .
In 1950 my primary school education ended. Almost without
noticing it, and certainly without any consultation between the
school and my parents I slipped into an academic course in
Portree Secondary School. Half my primary friends disappeared
into what was known as the practical stream. . .' A third recollects
her time in Motherwell 'Dalziel High, and a five-year Academic
Course. The best. Your father and mother said they had always
known you would. It was a good school. They kept telling you so.
It had wonderful playing fields, old traditions, an excellent
academic record which it was up to you as One of the Lucky Ones
to maintain. . .'

In 1965 the Labour government introduced six-year compre-
hensive secondary schools in Scotland as well as in England. This
made little difference to most omnibus schools, which altered

Language laboratory at Craigmount School, Edinburgh, in the 1970s.
By this time the emphasis is on learning to speak a language, rather
than just to read and write it. SLA

little other than their internal arrangements, and adopted structures very close to those proposed in the 1920s, then so brusquely dismissed by the SED. It was in the largest towns that the new policy had the greatest effect, with much reconstruction and much new building. Strange to say, the policy as applied there often exacerbated, rather than eased, social class divisions. The geography of large housing estates in the cities, of post-war council and private housing alike, which often became the catchment areas for new schools, tended to seal off children more than ever into their own, all-but exclusive communities. Proposals for two or three tiers of schooling, to stimulate social-class mixing by successively widening the catchments, were almost without fail refused. Indeed, the often very strict application of catchment boundaries and restriction of school-choice tempted many parents, who could afford to do so, to send their children (both boys and girls) out of the state system, into fee-paying yet comparatively inexpensive day-schools. In turn, these schools were often revitalized, became much more academic, and began to thrive, even before the Thatcher years. Nor were these the only consequences of a remarkable revolution in Scottish schooling which was begun in the 1960s.

11 Revolutionary times?

Pressure from the centre to reduce or remove social class inequalities in education, largely beginning with secondary schooling and driven mainly by English experience, was paralleled in Scotland with much reforming activity within schools, primary and secondary. The prime agency for change was the SED, where the power already lay: for example, since the 1950s, it had had effective control of all curricula. The existing centralization of educational planning and administration began to come under more exacting scrutiny from professionals and from a better informed and critical public. Not only was the direction of schooling in SED hands; it controlled the national examinations,

Saracen Primary School in Glasgow in 1974.

advanced education in commerce and technology (the Central Institutions), teacher training, the many further education colleges, and more. Only the universities stood outside its direct influence; but when an attempt was made to incorporate them under a single funding authority in the Scottish Office it was beaten off, more from deep suspicion of the SED than because of the claims that the Scottish universities could thrive only in a British, or rather in an international, context.

Yet that commanding sway over Scottish education was about to be relaxed, as a number of reforms were made in the management structure in the course of the 1960s. In 1963 a new Examining Board was set up to conduct new Scottish Certificate of Education exams. A new Consultative Committee on the Curriculum, in 1965, with its numerous national working parties, although also still under the wing of the SED, began quietly to loosen its hold on curriculum policy-making and planning. The General Teaching Council of 1966 weakened the direct grip of the Department on teacher education and the conditions of service for teachers. And the role – and the forbidding dominance – of the inspectorate was weakening too, as inspectors were forced to become advisers, working 'side by side' with teachers. Later, the Scottish Vocational Educational Council intruded on SED territory, providing certification for non-SCE courses in schools as well as in further education; and in the early 1990s the transfer of the Central Institutions into the university sector further ate into its old suzerainty. Greater freedoms for new school-based managements and innovations such as individual school budgets cut into old SED powers as well as into the controlling mechanisms of local education authorities. In short, the 1960s ushered in a period of insistent, demanding, often stumbling change, but change of a kind which had an impact not seen since the curricular revolution of the later eighteenth and early nineteenth centuries or since the restructuring that followed the 1872 Act. And, so it seems, it is not over yet. . .

12 Epilogue

The consequences of a return to the operation of 'market forces', attempts to enhance parental choice among different forms of schooling, improving opportunities to return to education after a break, however long, and removing rigid barriers between secondary schools and further and higher education, arguments for the particular long-term values in moral training in infant and nursery schools (and demands for places in them for all), debates over pupil 'disillusion' with schooling, over compulsion to attend and truancy, these 'live' questions and many, many more are all uncannily reminiscent of those being hotly pursued in Scottish education a century and more ago. But there seems to be remarkably little awareness of this. Since the 1960s there has been a plethora of reports from Departmental and Scottish Office committees on very varied aspects of Scottish schooling, with much drawing on the experience of other nations – in Europe (including England and Ireland), North America, Australasia – yet hardly a glance at, never mind an informed historical view of, the inherited Scottish experience. Too often this seems to be dismissed with some jejeune reference to the 'democratic tradition' (ineptly defined), almost as though there is nothing to be learned from the extraordinary and sometimes very revealing record of the distinctive Scottish past. Doesn't Scottish complex education, as has been rightly remarked, deserve to be developed with reference to its own society and its own living heritage, and not someone else's?.

Children at a nursery school in Jedburgh, 1933. SLA

FURTHER READING

We still await a good, modern history of Scottish schooling before the eighteenth century, but the better county histories of education are useful here. Among these, the most recommendable for the post-Reformation era and beyond are: J M Beale (ed D J Withrington) *History of the Burgh and Parochial Schools of Fife*, Edinburgh 1983; Alexander Bain *Education in Stirlingshire from the Reformation to the Act of 1872*, London 1965; William Boyd *Education in Ayrshire through Seven Centuries*, London 1961; I J Simpson *Education in Aberdeenshire before 1872* London 1947; There is much of interest in the two-volume *History of Scottish Education* London 1969 by James Scotland: vol 1 deals with the period before 1872, vol 2 with 1872 and its aftermath.

For the eighteenth century, see Alexander Law *Education in Edinburgh in the Eighteenth Century* London 1965, and D J Withrington 'Education and society in the eighteenth century' in N T Phillipson, R Mitchison (eds) *Scotland in the Age of Improvement* Edinburgh 1970, repr 1996.

For the nineteenth century, two outstanding contributions have been made by R D Anderson *Education and the Scottish People 1750-1914* Oxford 1995 and *Education and Opportunity in Victorian Scotland: schools and universities* Oxford 1983, new ed Edinburgh 1989. Most of the essays in W M Humes, H M Paterson (eds) *Scottish Culture and Scottish Education* Edinburgh 1983 have something arresting to say. Three good surveys, with new data and reinterpretations for the past two centuries, by D J Withrington (1750-1830), Helen Corr (1830-1914) and Andrew McPherson (since 1914) are successive volumes of *People and Society in Scotland* Edinburgh 1988, 1990, 1991, published for the Scottish Economic and Social History Society.

Studies of special areas include Marjorie Cruikshank *History of the Training of Teachers in Scotland London* 1970; T M Bone *School Inspection in Scotland 1840-1966* London 1988; T A Fitzpatrick *Catholic Secondary Education in South-West Scotland before 1972* Aberdeen 1986, and an account of the 'saving' work of industrial and reformatory schools, mainly in Glasgow, in Linda Mahood *Policing Gender, Class and Family, 1850-1940* London 1995. A sympathetic and knowledgeable Englishman's view of recent Scottish education is to be found in G A Osborne *Scottish and English Schools: a comparative survey of the past fifty years* London 1966.

Finally, there are telling insights into the Scottish educational experience in a wide-ranging study of the interrelationship of social and intellectual history with school ideals and practice in David Hamilton's *Towards a Theory of Schooling* London 1989: don't be put off by the title.

PLACES TO VISIT

Older school buildings are scarce in Scotland. Parish and other local schools in rural areas were very widely replaced after 1872, with some converted into houses or for commercial use. Reference to older Ordnance Survey maps show where the schools once stood or may still stand. Some later eighteenth-century and early nineteenth-century buildings are, here and there, still recognizable. A recent survey of twenty-six parishes in Upper Clydesdale has revealed only four wholly pre-1872 school buildings still identifiable: these include an 1815 building in the school at Carnwath, closed in 1980, and buildings dating from 1836 and 1844 at Lamington and Crawford respectively.

But there are older buildings in some of the burghs, and some, as in Montrose, are still in use within a newer school complex. The school buildings in towns which have remained to us from the seventeenth and eighteenth centuries are mostly those of hospital and charity schools, for which substantial endowments were left. George Heriot's in Edinburgh is one outstanding example; another is the Robert Gordon's College in Aberdeen. The ancient towns' grammar schools of Edinburgh and Aberdeen are marked in the street names of High School Yards and Schoolhill. Their nineteenth-century replacements were built elsewhere. Many smaller Scottish burghs still have their nineteenth-century 'public schools' built by their school boards: North Berwick's, in School Road of course, is now a local museum among other things, while the old High School is now the primary school, a new High School having been built in the 1940s on a greenfield site. This historical progression, still very visible on the ground, is mirrored in many other Scottish burghs.

Local museums are usually a good starting point for seeking out the history of schooling in the community. There are often old photographs, of buildings long gone, of classrooms, of teaching in operation, as well as class photographs of scrubbed and neatly-dressed pupils and rather forbidding-looking teachers. You may also find copies of class or examination certificates and citations for school prizes and newspapers cuttings of school openings or other notable educational occasions.

The carefully reconstituted classrooms and displays at Scotland Street School Museum of Education in Glasgow are well worth a visit. Designed by Charles Rennie Mackintosh, the building shows that not all local authority schools of its era were architecturally dull and barrack-like in atmosphere.

The new Museum of Scotland, which opens in November 1998, will contain material relating to education and learning in Scotland, from the Middle Ages to the twentieth century.